T0280006

SANXINGDUI AND CHENGDU

✦ THE BIRTH OF A MYTH ✦

www.royalcollins.com

SANXINGDUI AND CHENGDU

✦ THE BIRTH OF A MYTH ✦

Lin Ganqiu

Translated by
Wu Meilian & Mark Law

Books Beyond Boundaries

ROYAL COLLINS

Sanxingdui and Chengdu
The Birth of a Myth

Lin Ganqiu
Translated by Wu Meilian & Mark Law

First published in 2023 by Royal Collins Publishing Group Inc.
Groupe Publication Royal Collins Inc.
BKM Royalcollins Publishers Private Limited

Headquarters: 550-555 boul. René-Lévesque O Montréal (Québec) H2Z1B1 Canada
India office: 805 Hemkunt House, 8th Floor, Rajendra Place, New Delhi 110008

Original Chinese Edition © Chengdu Times Press Co., Ltd.

ISBN: 978-1-4878-1147-1

To find out more about our publications, please visit
www.royalcollins.com.

Contents

———◆◆———

Chengdu: Myth, Legend, and History

The great people of the Kingdom of Shu in southwest China worshipped stones. They originally lived in the "stone chambers of Mount Min" and were buried in stone sarcophagi (coffins) when they died. Later, they moved to the Chengdu Plain, with its wealth of rivers, and established splendid civilizations beyond modern people's imagination, represented by Sanxingdui and Jinsha. These civilizations gave birth to many myths and legends, such as "It had been thirty-four thousand years between the reign of Cancong and that of Kaiming" and "Cuckoos sing the sad songs of King Wang." The Shu people paid great attention to sericulture (growing silkworms and producing silk); thus, Song scholars referred to Chengdu as "the ancient Kingdom of Cancong (clusters of silkworms)." We may infer from the rich mythical legacy of the land of Shu that the history of Chengdu has always been intertwined with myths and legends.

About 3,200 years ago, significant human habitats such as the Jinsha site already existed in present-day Chengdu. It was much earlier than the time of the "City of Chengdu," where the ninth ruler of the Kaiming Kingdom reestablished its capital, as recorded in the *Chronicles of Huayang* or that of the legendary "City of Zhangyi" built after the State of Qin had annexed the Kingdom of Shu. However, it was unclear whether the site was named "Chengdu" and which king of Shu ruled it.

In his famous poem *Ode to Hard Roads to Sichuan*, the famous Tang Dynasty poet Li Bai exclaimed:

Cancong and Yufu founded a new state in the distant haze!

It has been forty-eight thousand years,

yet it is sparsely populated on this path to Qin.

A Liangzhu-style jade *cong* (cylinder-shaped ritual object) crossed the millennia of history, spanning ten-thousand peaks, and appeared within the Jinsha site; Shu did not communicate with the outside world, if not the poet's conceit, which was as exaggerated a legend as the 48,000-year-old or 34,000-year-old state throne.

According to *Supplementary Notes to the Classic of Mountains and Seas* by the Ming scholar Yang Shen, "The field of Duguang was by the black river in the southwest. It was where Houji, an ancestor of Zhou, was buried. (Note: the city was about 150 kilometers between heaven and earth)." Yang identified "Duguang" as Chengdu, thus showing "the land of Duguang" as Chengdu plain. Could the city of Duguang be the original Jinsha site?

We may find the earliest ode to Chengdu in the *Classic of Mountains and Seas* if such an assumption was accurate.

All crops grew there,

Both in summer and in winter.

The divine birds sang,

The phoenix danced.

The lingshou trees thrived,

Among all other plants.

And all animals,

That lived and prospered there.

The plants here never died,

in summer or in winter.

As absurd as the statement "never died, in summer or in winter" may seem, it refers to the evergreens such as those that the great Tang Dynasty poet Du Fu had seen when he visited Chengdu, "The trees were lush and green in winter."

In 316 BCE, the Qin army entered the Jiameng Pass via a stone cattle path, which, as the legend goes, was the channel built for transporting the gold-giving stone cattle into Shu that eventually resulted in its destruction. The Qin army hunted and killed the twelfth ruler of the Kaiming Kingdom, and the ancient Kingdom of Shu thus ended.

In 314 BCE, King Hui of Qin moved ten-thousand households from the State of Qin to Chengdu. After that, people's interactions and goods exchange among the states of Qin, Shu, and Chu in the south became more frequent.

In 311 BCE, Zhang Ruo, the first governor of the Shu prefecture, built a new city in Chengdu following the structure of the ancient Qin capital in Xianyang (near Xi'an in today's Shaanxi Province).

In 256 BCE, Li Bing became the new prefecture governor, and his official residence was near present-day Tianfu Square in Chengdu. In 2013, a stone rhinoceros was unearthed at the square, which provided evidence for the story of Li Bing building five stone rhinoceroses to tame the water demon.

A hydro project called *peng* or *lidui* in the Shu language began at the mythical site of the ancient kingdom of Yufu. It was the embryonic form of Dujiangyan, the source of the "heavenly province."

In 238 BCE, Chengdu first appeared as a place name on a bronze halberd under Lü Buwei's manufacturing supervision. (Not that earlier cultural relics with the name of Chengdu cannot still be found). It suggests that the public already knew Chengdu by then.

Chengdu was already a "heavenly province" more worthy of the praise of being "rich and fertile" than before, where the people took a healthy control and well used the river system.

Between 143 and 141 BCE, Governor Wen Dang created "the stone chamber of Mr. Wen" in Chengdu, considered the first local government-run school in China, and created a literary tradition in Chengdu.

In 144 CE, a stele was erected to commemorate the merits of Governor Pei Jun. On it were inscribed the words "one of the five cities," which implied the importance and prosperity of Chengdu as one of the five most influential cities along with Luoyang, Handan, Linzi, and Wan, as stated in the *Book of Han*.

In 166 CE, the Eastern Han government made "three divine stone figures" imitating the image of Li Bing and put them by Beijiangpeng—the official name for Dujiangyan at the time—with an intention for them to "tame the water forever," just like Li Bing's five stone rhinoceroses.

Ying Shao, the governor of Taishan Prefecture and a contemporary of the event, vividly described the tale of Li Bing changing into a bull and fighting the river god in his *Comprehensive Meaning of Customs and Mores.*

History, when exaggerated, becomes legends and myths. As Li Bing made the stone rhinoceroses harness the river, he became legendary and gave rise to the tale of a powerful local ruler who changed into a bull and fought the river demon for the wellbeing of his people. The stone rhinoceroses corresponded to Li Bing in the appearance of a bull, and the river god referred to the unruly tides. From history to myth, it is a through exaggeration that the shape and nature have changed.

What remains unchanged is Chengdu's magic, remoteness, and beauty. The cultural relics excavated at the Jinsha site represent the magic of Chengdu, the *Ode to Hard Roads to Sichuan* sings about the remoteness of Chengdu, and the *Field of Duguang* carries the beauty of Chengdu. Perhaps it is because Chengdu is so magical, remote, and beautiful that it has given birth to corresponding myths and legends. Over time, these myths and legends have been gradually incorporated into the long history of Chengdu, making it difficult to peel off and part with.

———— ◆◆◆ ————

Beautiful and Grand—the Meaning of Chengdu

As a place name, what does "Chengdu" actually mean?

Aside from modern research, such as "An Attempt to Further Explain the Naming of Chengdu" by Wen Shaofeng and "Agreeing to 'An Attempt to Explain Further the Naming of Chengdu'" and Chapter Two in *A Study of the Sites of City Walls of Chengdu* by Ren Naiqiang, the most authoritative study on Chengdu was conducted by Song scholars.

For example, Volume 166 of the *Imperial Reader of the Taiping Era* records, "According to the *Records of the Grand Historian*, King Tai of Zhou crossed Mount Liang and went to Mount Qi, where a city formed in one year, and a capital formed in two. Thus, it was named Chengdu (the formation of a capital)." However, the writing is more like that of *Prime Tortoise of the Record Bureau* than to *Records of the Grand Historian*. In Volume 407 of *Prime Tortoise of the Record Bureau*, it says, "King Tai of Zhou led his people across Mount Liang and stopped in the South of Mount Qi, built the city in Zhou. The Bin people were inspired by the benevolence of King Tai and came in droves to join them, and there were as many people as if they were going to a fair. In one year, a city was formed. Two years down the line, it became a capital."

In addition, in Volume 72 of *Universal Geography of the Taiping Era* it is written: "Because King Tai of Zhou traveled from Mount Liang to Mount Qi, [the place] became a city in a year and capital in two years. Thus, it was named Chengdu." It is probably a direct quote from *Genealogical Annals of the Emperors and Kings*, also mentioned in Volume 51 of *Broad Records of Shu*.

According to the second half of Volume 8 in the *Imperially Approved Detailed Outline of the Comprehensive Mirror for Aid in Government*, "Chengdu was the Ancient State of Shu. It became Shu prefecture under the Qin government and Yizhou Province under the Han. During the Jin Dynasty, it was changed to Chengdu State and then to Chengdu Prefecture during the Tang Dynasty. The name most likely came from the meaning of 'formation of a capital in three years' in *Records of the Grand Historian*."

Volume 51 of *An Exhaustive Overview of All Parts of the Empire* also supported this argument, "Chengdu's name most likely came from the meaning of 'formation of a capital' in *Records of the Grand Historian*."

The term "Chengdu" mentioned in these sources meant "becoming a city," which was the same as the usage in the Warring States period texts such as *Guanzi*, *Shizi*, *Zhuangzi*, *Shenzi*, and *Master Lü's Spring and Autumn Annals*. Some argue that *chengyi* and *chengyu* refer to the abundance of followers that can make up a *yi* (city) or a *du* (capital). Still, the description can quickly demolish such a statement in *Prime Tortoise of the Record Bureau* mentioned above.

In his *Shu Capital Rhapsody*, Jin Dynasty litterateur Zuo Si wrote, "Beautiful and grand, Chengdu was its name." "Cheng" means grand; as in Chu Suiliang's "Report to His Majesty on the Abolition of the Government's Official Capital and Strict Official System," "Grand oceans come from tiny streams, majestic mountains form by small clods." "Du" means exquisite, as in "There is the lady in the carriage [with him]" in *The Book of Poetry* (Shījīng 诗经), "[she was] indeed fine and beautiful." And "Grieving at the Eddying Wind" in *The Poetry of Chu*, "only a lady is beautiful forever." The explanations for these characters are also found in *Explaining Terms*, *Collected Explanations of the Classic and Tradition of the Annals*, *Little Erya*, and *Extended Erya*. Therefore, "Cheng Du," as a synonymous compound, refers to a grand and beautiful city, exactly as how Du Fu describes in "Chengdu Prefecture," "The crowded city was filled with splendid houses," "I cannot find peace here despite its loveliness," etc.

In other words, Chengdu, the capital of the last Shu dynasties, differed from the earlier "new capital" and Duguang. It was a much bigger and more well-established city, with a city wall that was 23 meters high and six kilometers long—

the same structure as that of the Qin Dynasty's capital city, Xianyang—a city of grandness and beauty. Presumably, except for a few writers like Zuo Si, most users throughout history did not fully understand the meaning of Chengdu's name, despite frequently mentioning it.

PART 1

THE KINGDOM OF CANCONG

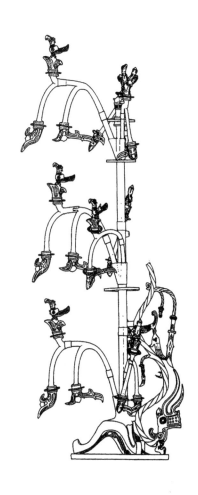

CHAPTER 1

———◆◆◆———

Chengdu, the Ancient Kingdom
of Cancong

In *The Golden Bough*, the groundbreaking work of modern anthropology, the author Sir James George Frazer says, "Myths are histories that are exaggerated." In a way, "transformed" may be a more accurate term. Myths, legends, and histories are connected mainly and intertwined.

The myths and legends of Chengdu provide us with access to the unique, eccentric aspects of the city aside from its daily lives.

"The capital of Shu was probably founded in the former dynasty." The "former dynasty" referred to the Ancient State of Shu, which was generally believed to be when the history of Shu began. It was a land of sericulture (the art of growing silkworms and producing silk), and Cancong was its first ruler. The stories of this mythical figure had always left the world wondering.

Who was Cancong?

Many writers have described the Ancient State of Shu in their writings. For example, in Li Bai's *Ode to Hard Roads to Sichuan*, "The Shu ancestors were Cancong, Bohuo, Yufu, Puze, and Kaiming. During that time, people wore their hair in a pointed bun and tied their collars to the left. They did not have any systems of writing, rites, or music. It had been thirty-four thousand years between the reign of Cancong and that of Kaiming."

As the texts described, no nation could last tens of thousands of years. These were essentially the poets' imaginations of the ancient kingdom that existed long before anyone could remember. Later, some people also stated that the first three rulers, Cancong, Bohuo, and Yufu, had each ruled for "several hundred years," which seemed more convincing as an actual state in terms of the years combined.

Who was Cancong? When did he live? Was he a man or a god? What did he look like? Where did he live? How did his life start and end? We can find approximate answers to these questions with a thorough reading of historical sources. Based on the *Chronicles of Huayang*, the earliest existing local chronicle in China, "The State of Zhou lost its social order, and the ruler of Shu took the lead in proclaiming himself King. Duke Cancong, with vertical eyes, proclaimed kingship. After he died, he was buried in a stone coffin, and his people followed this ritual. This was how the vertical-eyed people's tradition of burying in stone coffins began."

The Eastern Zhou Dynasty had lost much of its predecessor's prestige and social principles. With its deteriorating political status, its vassals one after another proclaimed themselves kings. It was not unlikely that the Duke of Shu was the first to undermine the Zhou's leadership because it was so remote.

We can probably predict Cancong's image based on the bronze mask kept in the Chengdu Museum: he had long and sharp eyebrows and pointed, apricot-shaped eyes with lowered eyelids. Based on *Qionglai County Annals*, Liu Lin believed, "Cancong's image most likely was derived from the blue-faced statues of deities consecrated in the State of Shu. They had a golden irregular bump like a silkworm on their faces and a vertical eye in the middle of their foreheads."

It must be such a horrifying site for a man to have a face with a blue complexion, bumpy skin, and a vertical eye. However, it was nothing strange for a god.

"Cancong originally lived in stone chambers in Mount Min." Some argued that the stone chambers were the Qiang people's military watchtower, frequently seen today in the Autonomous Prefecture of Ngawa (in northwestern Sichuan Province). The Canling Mountain in Mao County and the Can Cliff (or Canyan Pass) in Daojiang County (Dujiangyan) were both believed to have connections with Cancong.

Later, Cancong "became king at Qushang," a city near Mumashan at the junction of Xinjin and Shuangliu. Large numbers of cultural accumulation layers were discovered here during an excavation project at Mushan for irrigation in the

1950s.

Because the ordinary people of Shu followed Cancong in managing their funerals, the future generations considered graves with stone coffins that of the "vertical-eyed." One of the most important archaeological discoveries of the Eastern Zhou in Sichuan was tomb No. 1 in Mutuogou, Mao County, excavated in 1992. It was a burial site with high specifications in the upper reaches of the Min River in northwest Sichuan, with a stone coffin made of enormous pieces of flagstones laid in the tomb pit. The site contained bronze *lei* (large earthenware wine jar) and weapons with distinct features of the Shu Kingdom—perhaps they were also somehow related to the mysterious King Cancong.

According to legends, Cancong "... did not die but became an immortal. Many of his people went with him." It brings up the memory of the carefree, happy Monkey King and his little followers whose names were removed from the "Book of Death" and thus unrestrained by the world's rules.

Cancong Introduced Sericulture

"After Cancong became the king of Shu, he taught his people how to breed silkworms and raised several thousand golden-head silkworms." The name of Cancong was made up of two characters, *can*, which means silkworm, and *cong*, which means gather.

Cancong "used to travel in the field in black and teach people their business with the silkworms. The people were grateful for his merit and built temples to commemorate their king, where all their wishes were granted." There are many temples of Cancong, the "Black Robe God," in the land of Shu. For example, "there is a shrine for the black robe god that worships Cancong in Shengshou Temple in Chengdu."

"Because the ordinary people referred to [Cancong] as the black robe god, a county was thus named Qingshen, the Black Deity." Initially set during the Western Wei Dynasty and named Qingyi, the county was renamed Qingshen in the Later Zhou. In 1958, it was included in Meishan County as Qingshen District but regained its position as a county in 1962. In 1997, it was divided under the jurisdiction of Meishan District, and now it belongs to Meishan City.

"Every year, at the beginning of the year, Cancong would give each household a golden-head silkworm so their silkworms could proliferate. After that, the people would return these breed silkworms to Cancong."

"Later, Cancong stopped giving the [golden-head silkworms] to people. He gathered them and buried them by the river. It became a silkworm tomb."

"Wherever Cancong went, a silkworm bazaar would quickly form. The Shu people continued the business he started and opened a silkworm market every spring."

The Charming Silkworm Market in Chengdu

The silkworm market of Chengdu was the most famous and prosperous in the State of Shu.

There were many silkworm markets in Chengdu, probably even more than we could imagine, "During the first three months of the year, there were fifteen [bazaars] in the towns of the state and all other states around it."

Four of the twenty-one poems titled "Poems of Amusement in Chengdu" that Tian Kuang, the Chengdu governor in the Northern Song Dynasty, wrote were about the silkworm market. For the lunar month bazaars—"Silkworm market at the South Gate of the City on the fifth Day of first Lunar month" and "Silkworm market in front of the Shengshou Temple on the Twenty-third." For the second month's bazaars—"Silkworm market in front of the Daci Temple on the Eighth." For the third month, bazaars—"Silkworm market in front of the Daci Temple on the Ninth."

The Yuan scholar Fei Zhu from Shuangliu, Sichuan, described the bazaars on the fifth day of the lunar month—also called "five gate" outside the south gate—in *An Elegant Chart with the Record of the Seasons*. In addition, there were also bazaars on the fifteenth day of the second month. In *An Exhaustive Overview of All Parts of the Empire*, Song scholar Zhu Mu says, "In Chengdu, the ancient kingdom of Cancong, people took sericulture seriously. Therefore, they sold plants and silkworm facilities at silkworm markets." The traded goods at the markets were of a wide variety. As a Song Dynasty poem says, "The common people brought various goods to sell at the markets. They took the opportunity before the farming season [so that they could make some money] to help their work in the field. There were many goods, including the trifling type one could imagine."

In the third month, there were bazaars at the Long Bridge on the third. According to *Records of Chengdu* that Ye Tinggui quoted in *Detailed Matters Recorded Vastly as an Ocean*, "People from near and far all went to pray at the

Long Bridge on the third day of the third month. It was thus made a silkworm bazaar." In addition, "On the twenty-seventh, there were bazaars in front of Lady Ruisheng's Temple at Daximen. Originally, they were at the Xiaoshi Bridge and were moved to [Lady Ruisheng's] Temple after Sir Tian's prayer for rain was answered." Lady Ruisheng's Temple was the temple for the dragon king's daughter, which Gao Pan had relocated after establishing the city of Luocheng, and Xiaoshi Bridge was the Xiaoximenyan Bridge. Sir Tian Kuang, the governor of Chengdu, was well-liked by the Shu people, since he placed much emphasis on education.

The silkworm market in the third month was probably the most popular. "By then, all commodities could be found in the markets, and the streets and alleys were fully packed. It was a very grand and popular occasion for the Shu people." After seeing it, Su Shi's friend, the Song Dynasty monk poet Zhongshu wrote:

> Delighting in a visit to Chengdu,
> Joyful in the silk world,
> Hear the songs echo in the night.
> Shining lights on the red tower,
> I have been invited by Spring.
> Carriages and horses clog the streets in Yingzhou,
> As the crowd moves away,
> Silk merchants, blissful in the ring,
> As slender willows sway with mulberry leaves,
> My horse, without moving,
> Watches the bustling scene ...
>
> —ZHONGSHU, *Memories of Jiangnan*

It's a pity we can only imagine such glamour through his words today.

---•◆•---

CHAPTER 2

Sanxingdui and the God of the Shu

A bowl contains an ocean
Like two fish of yin and yang
The sun and moon circle around
Until the water dries up, the hills collapse,
The sea changes into a steppe
And the world changes into another
I will grow out a pair of wings in my mind
That wave upon the annual rings of the Sal tree
That brings back the memory of Shu

—Epigraph

The character *Shǔ* (蜀) appeared early in the oracle bone inscriptions in the Shang Dynasty, for example, "harvest at Shu," "a war against Shu," "arrive at Shu," "arrive at Shu on business," "Shu's defense," "Shu's army," "at Shu," "inform Shu," etc. But this term most likely referred to the "Shu" at Shandong. According to Du Yu's annotation of the *Tradition of Zuo*, "Shu was a place at Shandong. There was a Shu Pavilion northwest of Bo County at Mount Tai." "Shu" only became a specific pronoun for Sichuan when sources, such as the *Book of History*, *Strategies of the Warring States*, and *Records of the Grand Historian*, referred to Sichuan as Bashu, Jushu, and Yongshu. Some Warring States historical relics unearthed between the 20th century and now also contained words of "the

Governor of Shu ... Chengdu," indicating Sichuan. This evidence shows that the name Shu should have been confirmed no later than the Warring States period.

Shu has existed as a mature state in the Sichuan Basin since the Shang Dynasty. Writers of all time have mentioned the history of this mysterious kingdom in their works, including Yang Xiong's *Biographies of the Kings of Shu* in the Western Han Dynasty, Chang Qu's *Chronicles of Huayang* in the Eastern Jin Dynasty, Li Bai's *Ode to Hard Roads to Sichuan* in the Tang Dynasty, and Luo Mi's *Grand History* in the Song Dynasty. However, for a long time, these descriptions have been considered preposterous as wild legends rather than natural history. For example, the four sources all mentioned Cancong, the first king of Shu, with "a vertical eye" who later became a blue-face deity widely worshipped in the Shu temples, "With a golden irregular bump like a silkworm on his face and a vertical eye in the middle of his forehead." Was it true? Was he a god or a man?

In 1986, three bronze masks were discovered in sacrificial pit No. 2 of the Sanxingdui site, which seemed to solve the mystery of the "vertical-eyed."

The three masks were of varied sizes but with the exact modeling. They had square jaws, sharp, drooping eyebrows, and eyeballs stretched like cylinders outside the eye sockets. Most scholars believed the masks represent the deified Cancong's image. Cancong's kingdom was called Shu, the capital of which was the city of Qushang, "located nine kilometers south of Shuangliu County. There was a Qushang County at its north." It is worth pointing out that both characters, *qu* and *shu*, are formed with a radicle of "eye." According to *Increased Erya*, "Qu refers to a bird's action of raising and looking around after bending and pecking."

Coincidentally, the masks from Sanxingdui also feature an instant look of staring intently, except the face was not of a bird but of Cancong. He was the first king of Shu and the god to its people of all generations to come. *Unofficial History of the Scholars, Local Gazetteer of Hechuan County* (Newly compiled during the Republican time), and other texts thus referred to Shu as "Cancong's land."

Cultural artifacts related to Cancong have been found throughout history. Du Guangting said in "Story of Stalagmite," that Zhuge Liang had once discovered a piece of "King Cancong's stele for founding the country and taking an oath on Shu" on Zhusun Street in Chengdu. *Grand History* records another significant discovery in Chengdu in 484: "In the second year of Yongming, Xiao Jian was the governor of Yizhou. He [wanted to] build a Jiangnan-style Garden, so he [ordered to] break down a stone tomb with an outer coffin but without an inner one. In the tomb, he found several thousands of bronze vessels, three pots of jade ground into dust, tens of thousands of golden silkworm snakes, hills made of cinnabar and pools made of mercury, and uncountable treasures. An inscription was found written in seal characters that read, 'Cancong's tomb.'" After the Jinsha site—as a continuum of the Sanxingdui civilization—was excavated, these earlier unexpected discoveries, such as that of Xiao Jian's, were reexamined and given more significance.

On March 20, 2021, the conference on the progress of major projects of "China Archaeology" announced that silk for sacrificial purposes was discovered in the newest sacrificial pit at the Sanxingdui site. The silk, which undoubtedly came from silkworms, would probably draw the public attention to Cancong again.

Once again, the statement "myths are histories that are exaggerated" is proved credible by the archaeological discoveries at Sanxingdui that lasted for two centuries.

CHAPTER 3

———◆◆———

The Vertical-Eyed and Their Sun Worship

If you have not been hung
Like the chimes on the stand
If you never had a vertical eye
Like the telescope pointing at the stars
As the legend goes
Was it rouge or wrinkles
That adorned your face below
Was it worn out as the ages passed?
If you came from a foreign land
You should know a god
with a wing of a bird and a wing of a bat
He was known as Kronos in Greece
Saturnus, or Janus, in Rome
And Mithras in Persia, the god with the key
If you were born on this land
It would help if you still remembered the hands
that brought you to the world
You must have been yearning for the sun
During the long days buried in the dark

To challenge our assumptions and criticism
And break our mummified historical frame
Like wild horses, the lawless monkey king
who set havoc in heaven
Until the mystified truth is recovered
And our eyes will open wider than yours with shock
And you will clap your giant palms that were now lost
We shall know you
and know your warmth and smiles
to be the same as ours

—Epigraph

Sichuan, a poetic, heavenly habitat in the hinterland, is full of wonders. The name Sichuan also possesses artistic sentiments that often encourage romantic imagination. For example, Joseph Needham[1] explained the meaning of Sichuan as "Sichuan means four rivers, just like the Punjab in northwestern India, which means the place where five rivers converge. From east to west, these four rivers are the Jialing River (the largest river in Sichuan, whose upper waters are the route to the north), the Fu River, the Tuo River, and the Min River. Sichuan forms another natural region surrounded by mountains, which has repeatedly become an independent kingdom throughout Chinese history due to its privileged location and rich resources."

The Ancient Shu was the first of these independent kingdoms; in fact, the character *shu* does possess the meaning of "one" and "sole." The Sichuan polymath Yang Xiong believed "*Shu* means sole, unique, and not identical to others." People only understood what this sentence meant when the numerous strange but spectacular objects were revealed from the two Sanxingdui sacrificial pits in the 1980s, which genuinely dumbfounded the world.

The Dogs of Shu Bark at the Sun

The Ming scholars such as Yang Shen, Zhang Huang, Xu Yingqiu, and Lu Yingyang have already stated that "Sichuan's name came from the four rivers of

---

1. Joseph Needham et al., "Division I of General Introduction", vol. 1 of *Science and Civilization in China* (Beijing: Science Press, 1975), 124.

Minjiang, Tuojiang, Heishui, and Baishui." Although this explanation may not be etymologically accurate, it gives the correct geographical impression of Sichuan with abundant river systems.

When Marco Polo, the Venetian traveler, came to Chengdu during the Yuan Dynasty, he said, "I saw a water town almost the same as my hometown."

The Ming cultural geographer Wang Shixing from Zhejiang Province described Chengdu as "With clear, lovely rivers. Bridges, doors, and windows of people's homes are all built on the water, with shadows of pine trees and bamboo surrounding them above the waves. Everything is beautiful both on rainy and sunny days." Today, Sichuan is still referred to as "the province with thousands of rivers."

Aside from its rivers, Sichuan also has many mountains. According to Wang Shixing, "The vast and fertile land is surrounded by lush mountains on all sides. The Minjiang river and many others run across it and exit the basin from the Three Gorges because of the natural topography of the Sichuan Province."

Thanks to the favorable geographical environment, Sichuan is covered with dense green vegetation that blocks the sky. During the time of ancient Shu, rhinoceroses and elephants prospered on this land. These fierce, giant beasts that roamed side by side peacefully made the most spectacular scene of the primeval age.

The land of Shu, with rich water and dense forest, "rained constantly and had few sunny days. Whenever the sun came out, the dogs would bark at it." The people of Shu frequently suffered from floods, believing the disasters occurred because of evil water demons. Seeing the elephants play in the water without fear, they assumed their tusks had magic power that could tame the water. Therefore, they made special crosses with branches of large-fruited elms and tusks and threw them into the water, hoping to suppress "the demons." After "the demons" "died," the flood faded, and the once-submerged mountains were revealed again. This exorcise method was also recorded in the *Rites of Zhou*, which was probably related to the ancient people of Shu as well.

To tame the "water demon" with ritual objects, such as crosses made of elephant tusks or stone rhinoceroses, was called *yasheng*, which means to suppress people, things, or evil spirits with spells or prayers. The rituals of putting up couplets on Spring Festival and hanging mugworts on the Dragon Boat Festival that are still popular in China today also belong to *yasheng* practices.

However, the best *yasheng* exorcism was still inferior to the sun's power. We may still infer the joy of a nascent sun that shines and brings new hope upon the earth after the flood from the modern folk song of Sichuan, "Happy to see the sun come out."

Shu as a Ritual Object

The sun was the object of worship of all people in ancient Shu. Friedrich Max Muller, the founder of Western theology, claims that the sun god was the oldest god humans had created, and the Sun worship was also the earliest form of worship of all men. It was also the same for the ancient people of Shu.

Among the excavated objects at the Sanxingdui site, one was a Shang Dynasty bronze ware item that looked like a steering wheel, resembling the "sun pattern" on the bronze temple roof found in the same pit as well as that on the Sichuan hanging coffin tomb mural paintings and bronze drums in the south. It was thus named "Shang Sun-shape Bronze Artifact" or "Bronze Sun Wheel." Within the wheel are six identifiable individual components with diameters of about 70 to 80 centimeters. There were remaining traces of painting and piercing in the center and the outer circle of the wheel. It was probably a vital ritual object representing the sun often placed on the altar for worshipping occasions.

German scholar Hans Biedermann says in the *Dictionary of Symbolism*, "There are two types of icons representing the Sun, one is a circle surrounded by rays of light that are still used today, and the other is the 'sun wheel' with a longer history, a circle divided into four equal parts by two vertical crossing lines." But apparently, the "sun wheel" of Sanxingdui is a third category besides these two. The centerpiece that projects upward is like the Sun or a pupil, like the many eye-shaped bronze objects at this site. It is connected to the outer ring via five radial staffs that look like the beaming sun. It was either installed on the altar or held by priests or political leaders standing on top during sacrifices. "When the ruler follows the law of spontaneity, the world will be ruled by itself. Hold the sacrificial implement and give no orders; the government will be settled by itself." The term used to refer to the sacrificial implement that the *Guanzi* mentions here is *shu*, which can gather all people together by their faith.

The sun wheel of Sanxingdui reminds its viewers of the fairy tale "the Brother and Sister Who Guard the Sun and Moon," which is still prevalent in the Chengdu plain. Father Heaven had two precious possessions, the Sun and the Moon, which he locked in a cabinet. Father Heaven had a son and a daughter. They were very naughty children and always liked to go through their father's things. One day, they found the sun and the moon and happily went to play with them outside.

However, they didn't know that when they were playing with the shiny orbs in the sky, the earth below became bright, and plants, crops, animals, and humans began to grow. Later, a disaster broke out in the world when the heavenly siblings got tired and took the Sun and Moon back. The light disappeared, and everything lost its ability to live. The people kneeled and prayed to Father Heaven for the Sun and Moon, but the god was reluctant to give out his treasures.

At this moment, Lord Laozi said, "You shall give them out if the people need them so much. Otherwise, people will no longer respect you." Father Heaven thus brought out the Sun and the Moon and asked his children to guard them in turns, fearing they might be lost.

The bronze sun wheel must be a treasure as precious as the Sun in the eyes of the ancient Shu people. As the ages passed and the world changed, the Sanxingdui civilization disappeared with the wind. But the sun wheel stayed until today like the Sun it represented in the sky.

The "Vertical Eye" of *Shu*

The Shu people's eyes turned "vertical," probably because they had been looking forward to seeing the Sun come out too hard and for too long.

In the *Chronicles of Huayang*, "Records of Shu," the Chengdu historian Chang Qu recorded the beginning of the State of Shu as the Eastern Zhou Dynasty—which had underestimated the length of Shu's history. On the other hand, his fellow townsman and predecessor Yang Xiong and the great poet Li Bai, who praised Chengdu as "a place of heaven," claimed the State of Shu to be several tens of thousands of years old—which also had exaggerated the truth.

According to carbon-14 dating data, the recently excavated Sanxingdui pit No. 4 dated between 1199 and 1017 BCE, about the third and fourth period of the Yinxu site, or between 1123 and 1045 BCE, which was also much earlier than the Eastern Zhou Dynasty between 770 and 256 BCE.

For a long time, people have wondered and argued over the meaning of the "vertical eye." Some believe that it refers to a third eye in the middle of the forehead, like the Erlang Shen, while some consider it as eyes that grow outward, like the

Geji people in the Qiang myth. These people cannot see things straight unless they bend their heads. However, due to the lack of visual evidence, the accuracy of these assumptions is hard to prove. The writing of the upper part of the character *shu*, which indicates an eye (written as "ᗰᗰ" or "目"), largely remained consistent on the oracle bones, the bronze inscriptions, the stone-drum inscription, and the Han Dynasty texts. The oracle bone writing emphasized the eye radical the most and reduced the character's lower part into one curving stroke; some considered a worm or a dragon. There is another character from the Yinxu site, oracle bones with an eye radical and two "worms" below, which was also proposed as *shu* or its variation *zhu*. Experts have identified the writing of *shu* on the bottom of the grand human figure statues from pit No. 2. There are two characters inscribed symmetrically in a pattern that resembles that on the oracle bones.

What does *shu* mean? *Explaining Simple and Analyzing Compound Characters* describes it as "the silkworm (or worm) in sunflowers. It means worm. The upper part resembles the image of a silkworm's head, and the lower part resembles the image of its crawling body." Historian Deng Shaoqin, in the field of *Bashu* studies, points out that *Explaining Simple* was talking about the wild silkworm as the *zhu* in "Dongshan" in *The Book of Poetry*. "It was a great invention of the ancient Shu people to tame the wild silkworms into domesticated species, and so their king was referred to as Cancong." The name Cancong means "gathering silkworms," and this statement is supported by textual and archaeological evidence. In *Xian Zhuan Shi Yi*, quoted by Song Dynasty scholar Gao Cheng in *Compound Source of Matters and Facts*, "After Cancong became the king of Shu, he taught his people how to breed silkworms, and he raised several thousand golden-head silkworms. At the beginning of the year, Cancong would give each household a golden-head silkworm so their silkworms could proliferate. After that, the people would return these breed silkworms to Cancong. Wherever Cancong went, a silkworm bazaar would quickly form. The Shu people continued the business he started and opened a silkworm market every spring."

The description in *Xian Zhuan Shi Yi* offers insights into the origin of the silkworm market in Chengdu and the etymology of the character *shu*. The upper part indicates vertical eyes, and the lower indicates silkworm. Therefore, the character means Cancong with a vertical eye.

Cancong was a king of an independent kingdom, an advanced bronze civilization that existed long before the Western Zhou Dynasty. The bronze head represented his image—also called the bronze mask with "eye-idols" built in the late Shang period—65 centimeters high and 138 centimeters wide, weighing over 80 kilograms. Its eyeballs are made into cylinders with a diameter of 13.5 cm that stretches out of the sockets for 16.5 cm, which makes a most vivid and explicit explanation for "vertical eyes." It has large ears decorated with wild, curly cloud patterns with sharp, pointing tips like the top of a peach. This awe-inspiring image that suggests supernatural powers in seeing and hearing is undoubtedly a god's appearance rather than an authentic representation of a real person. It shows the deification process of Cancong, the ancestor of Sanxingdui, in the same way as the stone statue of Li Bing unearthed in 1974.

The "Vertical Eye" of *Qu*

The title of Cancong's Kingdom was Shu. There are two proposed locations for its capital city. One was Mount Min, and the other was Qushang.

The most popular opinion about Qushang was that it was in the Shuangliu District of Chengdu, but now new evidence shows that it was at the Sanxingdui site.

It is worth noting that the character *qu* includes two eye radicals, meaning it is also closely related to eyes. We may infer that *qu* refers to a pair of "vertical eyes" while *shu* refers to only one. Five eye-shaped ornaments, seventy-one eye-shaped utensils, and thirty-three *vesicula optica* were discovered in pit No. 2, and eye-shaped symbols and patterns were also seen on pottery from Sanxingdui. All these seem to suggest Sanxingdui as the ancient Qushang City.

With firm, upward-pointing eyeballs as long as 16.5 centimeters, Cancong's statue demonstrates the idea of *qu* to the fullest. Obviously, he was looking up at the sun. The abundant objects in the shape of eyes and the sun from pit No. 2 suggest that the worship of the sun and the vertical eye had existed together in Sanxingdui for a long time.

The Dogon people have an ode for their ancestors called the "song of the mask" that says, "masks, your bright eyes are the eyes of the sun." Coincidentally, this song is also an accurate description of the Shu people's worship of Cancong. Eyes, like the sun, are round and bright. That's why the eyes of Sanxingdui are always looking up to where the sun is.

—◆◆◆—

CHAPTER 4

Wangcong Temple

I n the southwest of the Pidu District of Chengdu, there is a Wangcong Temple
that worships two gods—King Wang and his successor King Cong of ancient
Shu. It is also the biggest imperial mausoleum and the only place for worshipping
the ancestors of Shu in southwestern China.

According to Qing research, there are two mausoleums where King Wang
and King Cong's swords and shoes are buried. This statement probably derives
from the allusion to the Yellow Emperor, "[the Yellow Emperor was] buried at
Mount Qiao. Suddenly, the mountain split open. There was no corpse in it, only
the king's sword and shoes." In other words, King Wang and King Cong became
deities like the Yellow Emperor and did not actually die. Their tombs were simply
monuments that later generations built to commemorate them.

The Man from Heaven

The third-generation ruler of Shu was called Yufu. The legend goes that his
territory was in Daojiang County, the site of which is now in Dujiangyan City.
"The ancient city of Yufu is about eight kilometers north of Wenjiang County."

One day, Yufu went hunting at Mount Jian, and he suddenly became immortal.
The Shu people thus built a temple for him there. At that time, the population
of Shu was small. "A man called Duyu descended from heaven to Mount Zhuti
(Zhaotong, Yunnan Province). A woman called [Liang] Li arose from the well.

[one day, when she] traveled to the river's source, Duyu fell in love with her and made her his wife."

After their marriage, "Duyu moved to the city of Pi, and the people of the former dynasty moved with him." According to *The County Annals of Pi*, "The old palace of King Wang was in the city of Pi, 25 kilometers north of the county. Duyu had been there before. During the Jin Dynasty, Li Xiong proclaimed himself governor of Yizhou and built his career there, too. Today, the palace has been abandoned."

It was natural that the people of Shu upheld Duyu, "the man from heaven," as their king. Very soon, Duyu succeeded Yufu and became the new king of Shu. "The seven states declared independence from Zhou, and Duyu proclaimed himself King Wang and changed his name to Pubei." In some sources, Pubei is recorded as Puze, but the former is more convincible, as the name of Pí 郫) probably came from the character bēi (卑). Some argue that Duyu "probably ruled Qushang," and he may have also built palaces there.

As his people and territory grew, Duyu "... believed his merit was higher than a king's. He thus made Bao and Xie his front gate, Xiong'er, and Lingguan his back door, Yulei and Emei his city walls, and Jiang, Qian, Mian, and Luo his ponds. Wenshan was his pasture, and Nanzhong was his garden." In *Shu Capital Rhapsody*, Zuo Si also wrote, "[Duyu] made Lingguan a gate and Yulei a roof. Two rivers ran through his territory like belts, and Mount Emei made natural protection." Bao and Xie refer to the Bao and Xie Valleys in Shaanxi. Xiong'er and Lingguan refer to Pingqiang Mountain in Qingshen County and Lingguan Mountain in northwest Lushan County. Yulei and Emei refer to Mount Yulei and Emei in Wenchuan County and Emeishan City. Jiang refers to the Min River, Qian the Qianxi River in northeast Guangyuan City, Mian the Mianyuan River across Deyang, and Luo the Shiting River in Shifang City. Wenshan is Mount Min, and Nanzhong includes areas in Yunnan, Guizhou, and the south of Liangshan and Yibin in Sichuan.

Duyu had indeed exceeded his three predecessors in expanding the Shu territory to an unprecedented scale.

King Wang and Cuckoo

A century after King Wang's reign, a serious flood was attached in the land of Shu. "Water came out from Mount Yu like the flood that broke out during the ancient sage king Yao's time. King Wang could not control it" (from the *Chronicles of Huayang*). The most recent flood at Mount Yu, or Mount Yulei, was in 1933 after the Diexi earthquake in Mao County, which the older generation may still remember.

When King Wang was feeling desperate, an expert in water regulation came from the Jingchu area. "After about a hundred years of King Wang's reign, a man named Bieling in Jing died, but his body was lost, and the Jing people could not find it. When Bieling's body floated along the river to Pi, he resurrected and met with King Wang. King Wang thus made him his prime minister." Of course, Bieling must have had a good command of water since he could "swim" in such a long way. Indeed, "When King Wang sent Bieling to tame the water, he quickly succeeded, and the people of Shu regained their peaceful lives."

Another saying holds that Bieling came from the well, like Duyu's wife.

However, "After Bieling went to tame the flood, King Wang committed adultery with his wife. The king felt ashamed and considered himself inferior in morals to Bieling. Therefore, he entrusted his throne to Bieling—like how Yao had entrusted his to Shun—and left the country." *Chronicles of Huayang* briefly stated that "The king went to the west mountain and disappeared there."

The west mountain was Mount Min, which included several famous mountains, such as Mount Qingcheng. Du Fu mentioned the west mountain in many of his poems, such as *Field Gazing, Ascend a Building,* and *Writing to Vice Governors Tao and Wang before Leaving Chengdu for Qingcheng.* He also had three poems titled *West Mountain* with the self-annotation, "Mount Min, the gigantic protection of all of Shu from the Qiangyi people." Even today, the local people of Dujiangyan still call the Daoist talisman at Mount Qingcheng "the west mountain writing."

In 641 CE, year 15 of Emperor Taizong's reign, the Tang Empire and Tibet were united through marriage, making Guankou (Dujiangyan) and Songzhou (Songpan County) a critical commercial path called "west mountain path" or "Songmao old way" today. The "west mountain" also refers to Mount Min, which stretches 711 kilometers from the Min County in Gansu Province in the north to Mount Emei in Sichuan Province in the south.

"The cuckoos were chirping when King Wang left. That's why the people of Shu found cuckoos singing melancholy as they think about their king." It was the sowing season when King Wang left, when cuckoos were most active. Interestingly, "cuckoo" is also closely related to "cuckold" in English, which people refer to as a male adulterer—"a cuckoo in the nest"—just like King Wang, who had sneaked into Bieling's chamber behind his back.

But why did the people of Shu commemorate a king with questionable morals? It was because King Wang had "taught his people to farm," and everyone respectfully called him "Lord Du," as they called Li Bing "Lord of the River." "The State of Ba also followed his teaching and committed its people to farming. The people of Ba and Shu still pay homage to Lord Du during the farming season today."

Slowly, the story of King Wang evolved into a legend. "King Wang cultivated *Dao* and became a recluse in the west mountain. There, he changed into a cuckoo bird and chirped in spring. His song was desolate and gloomy." Based on Zuo Si's writing of "birds with Duyu's soul," we may infer that this legend was well-known during the Western Jin period.

Today, there is another folktale on Mount Qingcheng related to King Wang and the cuckoo. Once upon a time, a beautiful cuckoo goddess lived in the Baiyun Cave and often went to a heavenly pool to bathe. One day, Duyu passed Mount Er on his military expedition and saw her. They fell in love, and Duyu gave upon her the title of Empress Guiyang. Sometime later, a coup occurred in the capital of Shu, and Duyu was murdered. His soul became a cuckoo bird and cried, "Gui-guiyang! Gui-guiyang!" all day and all night. Blood came from his throat and stained the azalea flowers in the valley red.

"Bieling succeeded King Wang's throne and became King Kaiming. He had two sons, Lu and Bao, who were also titled King Kaiming." The State of Shu thus entered its turbulent fifth dynasty.

CHAPTER 5

———◆◆◆———

The Business Street Boat Coffins —the Burial Ground of the Kaiming Dynasty

There is a large burial site with multiple coffins from the early Warring States period. The tomb was partly destroyed in the Han Dynasty. It runs from the northeast to the southwest, about thirty meters long and twenty meters wide. There are seventeen coffins in it in the shape of boats and canoes. Four are large coffins, with the largest reaching 18.8 meters long and 1.7 meters wide. Some of the thirteen small coffins were built for the people and funeral objects buried along with the tomb owner.

All the coffins were made of entire trunks of the valuable phoebe *zhennan* trees supported by multiple sleepers below. Both the coffins and the burial objects, such as lacquered woodware and bamboo mats, are well preserved, stuffed in thick layers of oxygen-proof activated montmorillonite clay. In the south of the tomb pit is a huge pillar base made of the head of a canoe. More importantly, there are tenoned square bar timbers 15 meters long and 7.5 meters wide connected to side compartments of the same size, both on the south and at the east ends of the pit. Scholars suspect these structures as architectural foundations, meaning that buildings were above ground on top of the tomb. Such an argument seems to testify to the architectural structure of temples and tombs, with "the 'living room' at the front and the 'bedroom' at the back" recorded in some texts, but had never been discovered in previous archaeological excavations. Based on the tomb specifications, we know that it may be an extremely rare cemetery of the Kaiming royal family or even the king of Shu himself.

Such is the basic information of the "large boat and canoe coffin burial site of ancient Shu" that surprisingly appeared on the business street of Chengdu in 2000, which was one of the ten major archaeological finds of the year for its unprecedented boat coffin scale.

What was the mysterious Kaiming Dynasty like?

Kaiming and Turtles

Kaiming, the founder of the Kaiming Dynasty, was a legendary figure.

King Kaiming was originally called Bieling (Biē líng 鳖灵), with two variations of the second character (lìng 夻 and líng 泠).

The names of the kings of ancient Shu were all related to animals. Kaiming was named after the soft-shelled turtle (bie), also called "round fish." Duyu "died and changed into a cuckoo," and his name also became the name for the bird afterward. Yufu was probably named after a cormorant that "every household in Kuizhou kept." This animal that looks like a duck (*fu*) is good at catching fish (*yu*) in the water with its beak, thus called *yufu*. Cancong, as mentioned previously, was named after the silkworms (*can*).

It is easy to relate these kings' names to their most remarkable merits or popular legends—Cancong taught his people to breed silkworms, Yufu made a living from fishing, Duyu retreated to the mountains when the cuckoos sang, and Bieling tamed the flood with his supernatural water skill. These animals were most likely what ancient Shu people considered possessing supernatural powers and viewed as their relatives, ancestors, and protection totems. They believed these animals could protect them and even give their powers out. To the ancient Shu people, totems were personified objects of worship. *Ling* means "god," thus *Bieling* means the "turtle god," and Bieling—King Kaiming—was the personified version of such worship.

In 1983, a bronze spoon with five painted images (see Fig. 1), including a turtle, bird, and fish, was unearthed in Sandong Bridge, Chengdu. The turtle is the biggest and occupies the center of the spoon. The bird and the fish are on the upper right and left hand corners next to the turtle, and the other two unidentified images are on the lower corners (the smallest one resembles a tadpole). The five

Fig. 1 The Bronze Spoon with Five Painted Imagines, the Warring States period, was unearthed in Sandong Bridge, Chengdu (Photo by Chengdu Museum).

animals are not painted according to their real-life proportions, suggesting that they were showing an abstract reference, status, and influence rather than actual animals. They are thus called "picture writing." The spoon dated to the Warring States period, which coincided with the Kaiming Dynasty. Therefore, the turtle may indicate Bieling, the bird may be Duyu, and the fish Yufu. The paintings may be a combination of ancient Shu people's totem and ancestor worship.

The Beginning of the Kaiming Dynasty

According to legend, Bieling's body floated to Shu from Chu, and he was resurrected. At this time, the land of Shu under King Wang's rulership was attacked by a severe flood, and Bieling was an urgently appointed job of taming the flood. He succeeded by breaking down the mountains so that the flood could go through, and Duyu abdicated and handed his throne to Bieling. This was King Kaiming or King Cong as known to the Shu people. Scholars usually refer to him as King Kaiming I, since his successors were also called King Kaiming.

King Cong's title may have some connection with the first king Cancong. Cancong promised his people clothes to wear, and Bieling provided his people land to live on—both of which were immediate, tangible benefits for their subjects. Many imperial rulers wished their heritage to be forever passed on but quickly failed. The Kaiming Dynasty witnessed twelve kings on the throne, while only the second and third kings were recorded in written history, "Kong Cong gave birth to King Lu, who attacked the State of Qin to as far as Yong (Fengxiang, Shaanxi). King Lu gave birth to King Baozi, who attacked the State of Qingyi, and his name was known in the land of Liao and Bo." The Qiang State of Qingyi was next to Xuzhou County near Yibin and Nanxi. *Liao* (liáo 僚 or liáo 獠) means hunting, indicating that the people of Liao lived on hunting. Bo both refers to Bodao County and the Bo people in Yibin. "In Bodao [County], there are weapon racks (or military camps) of the ancient king of Shu," says the *Chronicles of Huayang*. This statement provides a viable way to explore King Baozi's expedition to Bo.

"King Kaiming V, Kaiming Shang, began establishing temples in Shu. The country is called wine *li* and music *jing*. Red was the favored color. Kaiming Shang changed his title to Lord."

Pulling the Snake and Breaking the Mountain

"There were five giants during the Kaiming Dynasty who could move mountains and lift tens of thousands of weights. Whenever a king passed away, they erected a giant stone ten meters long as his tombstone. These huge 'stalagmites' were called Sunli. They were painted green, red, black, yellow, and white, with no written epitaph. Thus, the kings' posthumous titles also followed these colors."

In 337 BCE, the king of Shu—probably Kaiming Shang—sent an envoy to the State of Qin to express gratitude for the beautiful women he had received from Qin in the past. This time, the king of Qin again promised to give him five women, and the king of Shu sent the five giants to bring them back. When the group reached Zitong County, they saw a giant snake hiding in a cave. Out of curiosity, one giant quickly caught its tail, but he couldn't pull it out, no matter how hard he tried. Seeing this, the other four giants went up to help him. Then, disaster struck. The mountain collapsed and divided into five, killing the five giants and the five beauties as it fell. The king of Shu was overwhelmed by the sad news, and he condoned his unmarried wives on the mountains, which he named "five ladies' tomb mountains" or "five ladies' mountains." He built a fortress and tower on them to convey his longing for the ladies. Later, people renamed the mountains "five heroes' mountains" to express their respect for the five giants. "After the five giants died, their swords abandoned by the road immediately changed into spring. The spring changed back to the swords twice every sixty years on the days of *geng shen* and *jia zi*. Therefore, people named it the "spiritual spring" or "sword hiding spring."

Mount Wudan

The name of Mount Wudan, located in the northwest of Chengdu, probably derives from the story of "five (*wu*) giants carrying earth (*dan*) to build tombs into mountains." In addition, the Wuding Bridge and Wuding Street in Qingyang District may also be related to the same allusion.

In *Ode to Hard Roads to Sichuan*, Li Bai wrote:

> The Great Taibai rises in the west,
> A mountain where birds soar to their nests,
> Still, its crumbled peak bears a heavy toll.
> Five brave warriors lost. A sacrifice unfolds.
> When the earth crumbles, mountains fall,
> All the brave souls leave this world,
> Their spirit endures, a shining a light,
> A stairway to heaven, towering to new heights.

So far, we have known about the collapsing of the "five ladies' mountains." The tragic death of the five giants and will continue to explore the "ladder to heaven hooked the stone-wood bridge's side" as well as the history of Mount Wudan.

Opening the Golden Bull Path

According to Yang Xiong's *Biographies of the Kings of Shu*, "During the time of King Hui of Qin, Shu and Qin were at war, and Qin could not reach the land of Shu. [One day,] the king of Shu was hunting in the Bao Valley with tens of thousands of followers when he suddenly ran into King Hui of Qin. King Hui presented the Shu King with a basket of gold, and the latter also returned him with some gifts. However, [when King Hui returned to Qin,] the gifts from the Shu King turned into dirt. King Hui was furious, but his ministers bowed and congratulated him. 'Dirt is soil. Your Majesty will gain the land of Shu.' ... King Hui [thus] planned to attack Shu. He made five stone bulls, ordered special grooms to care for them, and put gold behind their backs. When the Shu people saw them, they considered them sacred bulls that could defecate gold. When the king of Shu heard about them, [he requested the bulls from Qin and was permitted] he immediately sent thousands of men [to accompany] the five giants as they dragged the bulls back to Shu. By the third bull arrived at Shu, a path was created between Qin and Shu. The Qin army, later led by Prime Minister Zhang Yi, was able to pass through thanks to the stone bulls." The path, later referred to as the "stone bull path" or "golden bull path," was the "ladder to heaven" and "stone-wood bridge" that Li Bai talks about in the poem. The Golden Bull District in Chengdu also received its name from this story.

The stone bull path became the primary passageway that connected the Guanzhong region and Sichuan from the Qin Dynasty to the Southern and Northern dynasties. The track originates from Mei County, Shaanxi Province, and links to Hanzhong through the Baoxie plank road. It goes westward from Mian County, exits the Yangping Pass, and reaches the Baishui Pass. It goes along the Bailong River valley to Jiameng, Shaxiba, and eventually to Jianmen via the Jiange path.

In 316, the fifth year of King Shen of Zhou and the ninth year of King Hui of Qin, Zhang Yi led the Qin army into Shu through the stone bull path and destroyed it.

Moving the Capital to Chengdu

"For eight generations after King Kaiming I, the kings of Shu established the capital at the city of Pi." This only changed during Kaiming IX's reign.

"King Kaiming (IX, or V in some sources) dreamed that the city was moving by itself, and he thus moved the capital to Chengdu."

Scholars have mostly agreed that the tomb on the business street belonged to the royal family of Kaiming, between Kaiming IX and XII. The young skeletons from the boat coffins—aged around twenty years old and under—suggested that these were adolescent royal members of the Kaiming Dynasty instead of the king of Shu himself.

Five Giants Built a Mountain

King Kaiming Shang was closely related to Mount Wudan.

In *Narration on Tang Dynasty Chengdu*, it is written, "King Kaiming Shang of Shu married a beautiful woman, originally a deity from Mount Wudu. When she died, she was buried in the northwest of the city, and the king sent the five giants to carry soil from her birthplace and build a tomb for her. Today, two pieces of rocks remain, and the saying goes that they were carried here by the five giants." This narration came from a more extended version in *Chronicles of Huayang*, "Records of Shu:" "There was a man—probably a mountain deity—from Mount Wudu who changed to a beautiful woman. The king of Shu saw her and made her his wife. But the woman was not used to the environment of the Chengdu plain and wished to leave. The king pledged for her to stay and even wrote the *Song of Dongping* to amuse her.

The empress soon passed away. Heartbroken, the king sent the five giants to carry soil from Mount Wudu to build a tomb for her. It occupied an area of several square kilometers and stood more than twenty meters above ground with a stone disk on the top. It was Mount Wudan, in the north of today's Chengdu. The king mourned his beloved here and wrote two more songs, the *Yuye Song* and the *To the Tune of "Returning to Long."* He buried the tomb makers himself [when they died] and erected a piece of tall rock to mark their cemetery. There was a rock like this in Chengdu with a perimeter of two meters and a height of about ten meters. Thirty kilometers north of the city, a rock like this was at Pi Bridge. Legend has it that these were where the five giants were buried."

There is another version of the story. The beautiful empress of the lecherous king of Shu was not a mountain deity, but the wife of an ordinary man from Wudu. It was probably a county in Mianzhu, like many other cities of ancient Shu whose names end in *du*, such as Chengdu, Xindu, and Guangdu.

Mount Wudan was also called "stone mirror mountain" because of the giant stone disk on top. During the Six Dynasties, Tang, and Song periods, there was a temple on the mountain called Wudan Temple, also known as Shijing Temple and Zhoutu Temple. Today, the mountain is in the Hanjianglu military area command yard of Chengdu and is no longer open to the public. But we can still see, as the "Records of the Shu" described, the mountain is not too big, about 20 meters high and 40 meters wide, occupying an area of 680 square meters. It is in the shape of a horse's hoof slightly tilted to the east, and its soil differs from the Chengdu plain. The stone disk is not to be seen now; only Du Fu's poem, *Stone Mirror*, proves its past existence.

> The king of Shu took this mirror,
> Placing it on the empty mountain
> when he saw her corpse.
> He pitied her sweet bones in the darkness of death,

She could grasp it in her hand
and bring it close to her jade-like face.
All the concubines sighed no more.
One thousand riders returned without her.
This heartbreaking stone, alone,
A buried disk under the moonlit vault.

The Ending of the Kaiming Dynasty

The Qin Dynasty's annexation of the Shu was a significant event in the history of Sichuan and Chengdu. As the *Chronicles of Huayang · Records of Shu* records, "In the fifth year of King Shen of Zhou, the Qin ministers Zhang Yi, Sima Cuo, and Duwei Mo [led the army of Qin] attacked Shu through the stone bull path. The king of Shu encountered them at Jiameng but lost. He fled to Wuyang and was killed by the Qin troops. The Shu prime minister, imperial preceptor, and the royal heir retreated to Fengxiang and were murdered at Mount Bailu. The lineage of Kaiming thus ended in its twelfth king's reign. In the tenth month that year, Qin defeated Shu, and Sima Cuo took over the land of Cha and Ba."

Jiameng was the name of an ancient mountain pass in Zhaohua County in Guangyuan. This was where King Kaiming XII lost the war, and Pengshan, Meishan, was where he lost his life and his kingdom. Fengxiang and Mount Bailu, where his son and followers died, were in Pengzhou.

Although the Kaiming Dynasty ended, the royal family did not die out. Historian Xu Zhongshu believes that "After the Qin subjugated the State of Shu, the descendants of the king of Shu and their followers scattered in western Sichuan and moved south along the Qingyi River, the Ruo River (Yalong River), and the Hengduan Mountains. They changed their names according to the place names where they stayed." The Qin army could not track them down and kill them all.

Compared to Kaiming XII, whose life ended violently and humiliatingly, the royal members who lay peacefully in the boat coffins were more fortunate.

CHAPTER 6

————◆✦◆————

The Soul-Carrying Boat

To make a boat, you will need to cut down a giant Chinese cedar, cut off the branches, peel off the bark, polish the trunk, cut it into two-thirds of its original length, take out the inner part, and bevel the end of the box from the bottom up to make it upswept. To make a boat coffin, you'll need two boats and put one on top of another with the bases facing out.

Between July 2000 and January 2001, archaeologists found a large cemetery site with multiple coffins on the Chengdu City center's business street. These boat coffins that came in varied sizes were orderly placed on blocks when they were excavated.

There are a total of seventeen coffins, four over ten meters long. The biggest is 18.8 meters long and 1.7 meters wide, made of an entire cedar trunk, which is also the most extensive boat coffin ever discovered in China. The other thirteen coffins are small and designed for the people and objects buried along with the tomb owner. Two of them are on display in the Chengdu Museum. One is about 4.77 meters long, 0.9 meters wide, and 1.08 meters tall. It has a lid and contains some pottery and lacquer wares. The other is about 4.53 meters long, 0.9 meters wide, and 0.6 meters tall. It doesn't have a lid, and its content includes bamboo baskets, mats, straw rain capes, and lacquerware.

When were these boat coffins made? Who was their owner? Why were they made into such particular shapes? And what can we infer from its location?

A preliminary conclusion indicates that the tomb belonged to one of the kings of Shu and his family during the Warring States or the later period of the Kaiming Dynasty, about twenty-five hundred years ago.

As mentioned above, King Kaiming I Bieling, the founder of the dynasty, was an outstanding legendary figure. Two sources of the Western and Eastern Han dynasties, *Biographies of the Kings of Shu* and *Comprehensive Meaning of Customs and Mores*, quoted in Volumes 56 and 888 of *Imperial Reader of the Taiping Era*, mentioned the story of him coming to the land of Shu along the river, resurrecting, and saving all people of Shu from the flood. His reputation was so distinguished that King Wang made him his successor and entrusted him with his country and people.

The discovery of the boat coffin at Business Street was not the first nor the earliest in Chengdu.

In 1987, archaeologists found a boat coffin tomb of the Warring States period at a Qingyang neighborhood construction site where an exquisite bronze bottle was unearthed. The vivid painting of a feathered man rowing a boat provided valuable material for studying the living and producing habits of the ancient people of Shu.

French scholars believe the painting shows a "soul-delivering boat" similar to the "golden boat" of the Dayaks on Kalimantan Island that sends the deceased's soul to heaven. Chinese scholars agreed that boat coffin burial was popular in the Shu area, probably relatable to the belief of sending off the deceased along the water.

In 2007, many boat coffins were found in the Jinsha No. 4 burial area at the Huangzhong Village, which testified to the usage of boat coffins in Chengdu as early as in the mid-Western Zhou period. Unfortunately, these coffins were in bad condition when they were found. They were in similar shapes to those in Business Street, but much smaller, mostly around one or two meters in length. The burial objects were mainly simple handicrafts, such as earthen pots. Experts believe these coffins were most likely for ordinary people instead of royalty.

Where did the souls of the Shu people go? Was it heaven, hometown, or somewhere else? In the *Biographies of the Kings of Shu* is recorded a place called Tianpeng Gate, where the souls of dead people would pass through. The gate consists of two mountains on both sides of the Min River, near Xuankou in Wenchuan County. Apparently, the souls were crossing the gate to reunite with their ancestors in the Chuanxibei Plateau, the birthplace of King Cancong, as well as the ancient Shu civilization. The boat coffins were the vehicles that carried them on their last journey in the water.

The boat coffins had a long history among several southern ethnic groups in China. There were two major categories of this burial ritual: open-air burial (hanging in caves or on trees) and ground burial.

The earliest boat coffins were the two boat coffins on the cliffs of Mount Wuyi in Fujian Province. These more than 3,100-year-old boat coffins were basically the same as the fishing boats used in the Hokkien regions. Similar to the boat coffins at Chengdu Business Street, they were also made of entire tree trunks comprising a lid on top and the main body of the coffin on the bottom. The lids were semicircular, and the corpse-containing space was rectangular.

Similar boat coffins were found in Hainan, Hubei, Hunan, Guangxi, and Guangdong provinces. They were known by multiple names, including "shabby skiff," "lignaloo boat," and "divine boat."

The boat coffin as a ground burial set was considered unique to the Ba people between the end of the fourth century BCE to the end of the first century BCE due to the constant excavation in the Three Gorges and Eastern Sichuan regions since the 1950s. However, from 1954 to 2017, ground burial boat coffins had also been discovered in various locations outside the ancient Ba habitation, including Baxian (Chongqing), Zhaohua, Guanghan, Shuangliu, Lushan, Pengxian (Pengzhou), Qiongjing, Dayi, Mianzhu, Shifang, Xindu, Pixian (Tuodidu), Pujiang, and Qingbaijiang. In addition, the large burial site at Business Street showed boat coffin burial was also popular among the Shu people.

In the Ming Dynasty, the land of Chengdu was rich and fertile, containing more than thirty states. There were "clear, lovely rivers. Bridges and doors and windows of people's homes [were] all built on the water, with shadows of pine trees and bamboo surrounding them above the waves. Everything [was] beautiful both on rainy days and on sunny days." Water played an essential part in Sichuan people's lives for a long time. In 1665, there was still water in the Moke Pool, which was only filled in 1914. In 1958, elementary students in Chengdu still had the tradition of holding boat rowing competitions in the city moat. We may imagine what a dense network of rivers there used to be on the Chengdu Plain in the time of the ancient Shu and how its people used to live by these rivers with their valuable boats as a vital means of living. Because of their attachment to the boats, they were buried in them when they died, eventually becoming a burial tradition.

As Karl Marx pointed out in Lewis Henry Morgan's *Ancient Society,* to make sure that the deceased enjoy the same kind of living and entertainment after their death, people often "Put everything that the dead owned and considered precious in her life into her tomb so she could continue using them after death."

Therefore, only people with profound connections to the boats would take the trouble to build their coffins into boats. It is worth noting that the small canoe coffins were made entirely according to the practical principles of daily use. Thus, we can assume that these coffins were originally boats and canoes that the tomb owners used during their lives. The *Excavation Report on Sichuan Boat Coffins* released by the Sichuan Museum states, "Either the coffins were practical vehicles or specially made burial sets. They display an intimate relationship between the local residents and the rivers. Using boats as coffins suggests a belief in the water as home or a need for boats after death."

Nevertheless, aside from in the Ba and Shu regions, boat coffins were not commonly used for burial in pre-Qin times. This tradition was thus a particular reflection of the local people's soul-delivering ritual and living habits. The abundance of boat coffins in Chengdu was not surprising since it had been the capital of Shu probably as early as the Jinsha site was built, and, if not, no later than King Kaiming IX's reign.

CHAPTER 7

Governor Sili before Governor Bing

The king of Shu's era ended with the merging of Qin and Shu, and Chengdu officially became the capital of Shu Prefecture in the State of Qin under the shared governance of the Duke of Shu and the Governor of Shu. *Chronicles of Huayang* states, "In the first year of King Nan of Zhou, King Hui of Qin appointed his son Tongguo as Duke of Shu [...] and Zhang Ruo the Shu governor. [...] thirty years later, Duke Wan was suspected of rebellion, and King Zhaoxiang of Qin executed him. [He canceled the position of Duke of Shu and] only kept that of Governor in Shu [...] After the State of Zhou collapsed, King Xiaowen of Qin appointed Li Bing as the Governor of Shu."

Who was the governor that King Zhaoxiang kept? His name was forgotten for over two thousand years until 2017, during the archaeological excavation of two Warring States royal tombs at Poliu Village, Qinhan New City of Xixian New Area, Shaanxi Province. Neither of these tombs had been robbed. The smaller one contained a double burial set with an inner and outer coffin. The funeral chamber consisted of an upper and side case, where large quantities of animal skeletons and over forty funerary objects were found. The larger tomb consisted of a tomb passage to the pit tomb and a funeral chamber and contained a triple burial set with one inner coffin and two outer coffins. There were many wooden boxes for burial animals under the tomb passage. The upper case of the funeral chamber contains one hundred and fifty-five funerary objects, including one bronze mirror.

In November 2019, the Shaanxi Academy of Archaeology identified the sixteen characters inscribed on the mirror as "nineteenth year [of King Zhaoxiang of Qin,] made under the supervision of Governor Sili, designed by Luo, the Engineer; managed by Qiucheng, the Assistant Officer; and made by Nai, the craftsman. The inscription follows the standard format of a joint signature of three rank titles of the time, which was convenient for accountability at all levels in case of quality issues.

According to *Records of the Grand Historian*, "General Sili attacked the State of Qi with the States of Han, Zhao, Wei, and Yan in the twenty-third year of King Zhaoxiang's reign. [Zhang] Ruo, Governor of Shu, attacked the State of Chu in the thirtieth year." We can infer from this account that Sili was Governor of Shu in the nineteenth year but had already resigned from his post in the twenty-third year. In the thirtieth year, Zhang Ruo became the governor again.

Records referred to Zhang Ruo and Li Bing as "Governor Ruo" and "Governor Bing" in accordance with the title of "Governor Jin (or Xuan)" inscribed on a bronze halberd from the ninth year of King Zheng of Qin's reign in Qingchuan and "Governor Wu" on another halberd from the twenty-sixth year of Qin Shi Huang's reign in Peiling. These references all followed the format of official titles of the State of Qin in the Warring States period. In this light, the inscription of *"shushou sili"* should also refer to a Governor of Shu named Sili marked by Zhang Shoujie in *The Proper Explanation of the Records of the Grand Historian*, "Wei means the title of general, and Sili was his name." the *Records of the Grand Historian* and *Chronicles of Huayang* probably missed his name (as well as Governor Jin's and Governor Wu's) due to the short term of his position that overlapped with the time of employment of the more well-known Governor Zhang Ruo. In addition, because King Xiaowen of Qin died in the first year of his reign, some scholars suspect the statement of "King Xiaowen appoint[ing] Li Bing Governor of Shu" in the *Chronicles* was mistaken. They believe that "it obviously took many years for Li Bing to overhaul water conservancy in Sichuan. Therefore, Li Bing was appointed as the Governor of Shu in the later period of King Zhaoxiang." Nevertheless, theoretically, King Xiaowen could still give the order during his reign—no matter how short it was—and Li Bing could still retain his position and accomplish his duty as Governor of Shu after King Xiaowen had died.

The discovery of the inscription that read, "nineteenth year [of King Zhaoxiang of Qin,] made under the supervision of Governor Sili" has testified to the reliability of *Chronicles of Huayang* and filled a gap in our understanding of Chengdu history.

A Brief List of the Governors of Shu in the State of Qin

From 316 to 206 BCE, the Kingdom of Qin ruled Shu for 110 years, and only six are known today. Among them, Zhang Ruo and Li Bing are the most well-known and have complete names, while the rest have either lost their surnames or their names, and their deeds could be better known. What is certain is that Zhang Ruo was the first, and Zhang Han was the last. As for whether there were only four terms between these two, namely Governor Sili, Bing, Jin, and Wu, it is too early to say for sure.

Name	Position	Term of office	Major deeds	Remarks
Zhang Ruo	Governor of Shu	314–? 277 BCE	He served twice as the Governor of Shu and destroyed Bashu. He built Chengdu City.	There is a goblet in the Shaanxi History Museum with the text "Thirty-four Years of Governor of Shu," probably from 273 BCE (the 34th year of King Zhao of Qin), and it is not known whether this governor is Zhang Ruo or another anonymous person.
Sili	Governor of Shu	288 BCE	In the 19th year of King Zhaoxiang of Qin, when Sili was the Governor of Shu for twenty-three years, he was reappointed as a commandant.	The surname is unknown but is the same as "Commandant Sili" in *The Annals of Qin* in the *Records of Grand Historian*.
Li Bing	Governor of Shu	250 BCE–?	Li Bing repaired Dujiangyan and governed Shu.	The time of Li Bing's service is more controversial. This book adopts the record of *Chronicles of Huayang*, "King Xiaowen of Qin took Li Bing as the Governor of Shu," such as the *Chronicles of Raozhou Prefecture* in the Kangxi Reign, "Li Bing ruled Shu in the Era of Duke Xiao of Qin," but this is based on a false rumor.
Jin	Governor of Shu	238 BCE	Not in detail	The surname is unknown. The word "Jin" may be pronounced as "Xuan."
Wu	Governor of Shu	221 BCE	Not in detail	The surname is unknown.
Anonymous	Governor of Shu	Not in detail	This person was appointed by Zhang Han (?–205 BCE), so his appointment should have been made before 205 BCE. He was killed by Lin Zhi (a marquis in 200 BCE), so his death should be happened before 200 BCE.	All names are unknown. See in "Yearly Table of the Officials Who Became Marquises in the Time of Gaozu" of the *Records of Grand Historian* and "Table of Meritorious Officials during the Reigns of (Emperors) Gao, Hui, Wen and Empress Gao" of the *Book of Han*.

PART 2

THE HEAVENLY PROVINCE

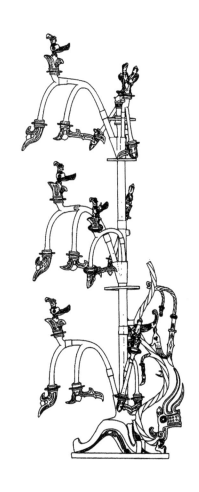

CHAPTER 8

———◆◆◆———

Dujiangyan before "Dujiangyan"

Foreword: The Fertile Land with Taro Roots

Before the Lidui Mountain was cut, I heard,
The river was wide without boundaries.
It ran straight across the land to the southwest,
And the people in Pi often lament their fate of drowning.
>   —the Qing Dynasty scholar CHEN BINGKUI from Guan County,
>   *The Song of Dujiangyan*

In 541 BCE, Liu Dinggong sang:

How marvelous and long-lasting Yu's merit was!
We would all be fish (drowned) if not for Yu!

The Min River at that time was one mainstream, as *Strategies of the Warring States* describe:

In the west of the State of Qin were Ba and Shu. Grain boats traveled along the thousand-kilometer water route between Mount Wen and the city of Ying. Ships that carried fifty passengers and a three-month provision could travel more than 150 kilometers a day. In summer, small boats could travel downstream and arrive at Ying in five days.

Mount Wen is Mount Min, and the river means the streams of the Min River and Yangtze River. We can thus imagine how wide and deep the Min River used to be before the excavation of Mount Lidui. In the river, there were "many tortoises and crocodiles," and in the mountains ashore, there was "much gold and jade. The vegetation was mostly plum blossoms and Chinese crabapple. Rhinoceroses, elephants, the legendary *kuiniu*, and golden pheasants were abundant."

In addition, according to *Records of the Grand Historian*:

> The ancestors of the Zhuo family in Sichuan, originally from the State of Zhao, became wealthy from their iron smelting business. After Qin destroyed the State of Zhao, the Zhuo family was forced to leave. They were taken captive, and only a husband and wife pushed their carts toward the designated relocation site. Those who were forced to move at the same time, as long as they had some money, were scrambling to bribe the officials who led the group, asking to be placed in a slightly closer place, settling in the area of Jiameng Pass. Only Zhuo said, "This place is small and barren. I heard that there is fertile land below Mount Min, and the land produces big taro roots, so we can feed ourselves and not die of hunger. The residents there are good at trading and easy to do business with." Therefore, they requested to be relocated farther away.

The praise for the "fertile land" spread after Shu's flood was tamed, and that was probably how the Zhuo family learned about the plain in the middle and lower reaches of the Min River. The big taro roots that grew there were called *dunchi*, and they received the name for their shape, which looked like squatting owls. A local ballad also went: "No hunger during the famine, thanks to the *dunchi*, no chaos during droughts, thanks to Guanghan."

The taro roots probably existed before the construction at Mount Lidui, but they certainly flourished afterward. Chen Bingkui continues his poem with the following lines:

> King Li built the Dujiangyan and opened the Jian River.
> Those thousand miles of fertile land, the people are happy to cultivate.

After Dujiangyan was built, farmers no longer needed irrigation machines in their paddy fields. It's no exaggeration to say that we should give all the credit to Dujiangyan for the "fertile land that stretches thousands of miles in the heavenly province" that Zhuge Liang mentioned in "Longzhong Plan." "The numerous streams join, and the several hundred miles of fertile land all came from the governor," wrote Chen Yaosheng, Director of the Collection Bureau of Guan County in the Republic of China.

In the following chapter, we will find out more about the Governor.

Western and Eastern Han: Cutting the Mountain and Dredging the River

Governor Bing—the Mo River

So far, the earliest written records to which we have access about the great Dujiangyan date from the Han Dynasty.

In "Treatise on Rivers and Waterways" (*héqú shū* 河渠书) of the *Records of the Grand Historian*, Sima Qian wrote: "Ever since Yu the Great had tamed the water, the rivers were dredged, and the lakes were cultivated. He pacified the states on the land of Huaxia, and his merit had benefited the three dynasties [of Xia, Shang, and Zhou]." After that,

> People diverted the [Yellow] River to the southeast from Xingyang and built a wide canal, which went through the states of Song, Zheng, Chen, Cai, Cao, and Wei and connected with the river systems of the Ji, Ru, Huai, and Si Rivers.
>
> In the State of Chu, the Han River and the Yunmeng Lakes were connected in the west, and there were canals connecting rivers in the east as well.
>
> In the State of Wu, canals were built among the three rivers and five lakes.
>
> In the State of Qi, canals were built between the Zi and Ji Rivers.
>
> In the Prefecture of Shu, Governor Bing cut Mount Lidui to prevent harm to the Mo River. He also opened two tributaries in Chengdu.
>
> These canals were all used for shipping and were sufficient for irrigation, benefiting all coastal residents, who often built uncountable small canals to

water their fields. But these irrigation constructions should have been more trivial to be mentioned.

Ximen Bao diverted the Zhang River to water Ye County. The Henei region of the State of Wei thus became prosperous.

The ruler of Han heard that the State of Qin was planning military attacks, and he wished to stop it from expanding eastward. Therefore, he promptly ordered Zheng Guo, a hydraulic engineer, to persuade [the ruler of] Qin to build a canal for irrigation from Zhongshan to Hukou, about a hundred miles to the east, that eventually joined the Luo River. [The ruler of] Qin discovered his intention in the middle of the project and was about to kill him. Zheng Guo said, "I was indeed a spy, but the canal will play to the benefit of Qin."

The king agreed and ordered him to complete the project. By then, the muddy water of the Jing River flowed over forty thousand hectares of saline-alkali land and cultivated one *zhong* of grain per *mu*. Since then, the Guanzhong region has had fertile soil and no famine. The State of Qin became more powerful thanks to the canal and eventually annexed all other states. The canal was later named Zheng Guo's Canal.

Despite the narration in the *Records*, Li Bing's water regulation projects took place later than Ximen Bao's but before the construction of Zheng Guo's Canal. Like the *Records*, sources such as the "Treatise on Rivers and Canals" (*gōuxù zhì* 沟洫志) in the *Book of Han* and *Eulogy of Fanhui Canal of Jingzhao* in *Literary Records of Eastern Han* by Cai Yong also placed little emphasis on the chronological order of these events.

Li Bing served as the Governor of Shu of the State of Qin during the Warring States period. Based on the inscriptions on Qin Shi Huang's bronze halberds with the words "Governor Jin" and "Governor Wu" as well as the *Records* mentioning of "Governor Ruo," we may infer that "Governor Bing" was the official title for Li Bing in the time of Qin. In *Engraving and Preface of Fulongguan, Which Was Relocated from Mt. Lidui* written by the Song Dynasty scholar Feng Kang, "Treatise on Rivers and Waterways" (*Hequshu*) is referred to as "Rivers and Canals, the History of Qin."

Aside from the consideration for rhetoric and rhyming of the sentence, it may also suggest that the mentioning of "Governor Bing" derives from a certain book of Qin history, probably the *Book of Qin* that Sima Qian had read.

The Governor in Qin's time was called *shou* or *taishou*. Many sources have mentioned this position. For example, *Qin Law Code "Fengzhenshi,"* Chapter "Qianzi," excavated from Shuihudi in Yunmeng County (Hubei Province), states, "[...] sent an official to bring the criminal to the Governor of Chengdu (Shu) with a permit and a letter across the states and gave them food according to the law." In *Comprehensive Meaning of Customs and Mores*, later quoted in *Commentary to the River Classic, Classified Collection Based on the Classics and Other Literature, The Proper Explanation of the Records of the Grand Historian*, and several volumes of the *Imperial Reader of the Taiping Era*, the event of "King Zhaoxiang of Qin appointed Li Bing Governor of Shu" is recorded.

At a time when men enjoyed absolute social privileges, men were referred to by their clan's name (*shi*) and given name (*ming*).[1] For example, Duke Zhou was known as Zhou Dan or Duke Zhou Dan. Qin Shi Huang, whose clan's name was Zhao and whose family name was Ying, was called Zhao Zheng. To refer to someone simply by his given name was also common, such as "Teng" as a self-proclamation in "Nan Prefecture Governor Teng's Document" or "Governor Qiang of Nan Prefecture reported" in *Judicial text Zouyanshu* from Zhangjiashan.

The records about Governor Bing in Ban Gu's "Treatise on Rivers and Canals" (*Gouxuzhi*) in the *Book of Han* are like that in the "Treatise" (*Hequshu*) except for the changes such as "Governor Li Bing." Some scholars argue that the *Book of Han* is the earliest source that confirmed this family name, and the documentary *Governor Bing* directed by China Central Television, states the later generations learned this family name from the inscription on the Eastern Han statue. But these statements were apparently wrong because the *Biographies of the Kings of Shu* had already mentioned it beforehand. In this case, Sima Qian, who must have known Li Bing's family name by the time he composed the *Records of the Grand Historian*, left it out on purpose to follow the tradition of the official titles of Qin—the same case in "Eulogy to Zhou Fujun, Prefect of Guiyang County of Han" composed in 174, the third year of the Xiping era.[2]

Both *The Six Tablets of the Masters Bai and Kong*, Volume 7 and *Imperially Endorsed Categorized Boxes of the Yuanjian Studio*, Volume 37, quoted from the

---

1. There are some exceptions to this tradition. For example, the military officer Wu Yuan was referred to as Shen Xu, combining his fief and courtesy names.

2. The year follows the statement of *Bronze and Stone Inscriptions*, Volume 1, and the title follows that in Volume 16. In Volume 4 of the *Analysis of Writings in Chancery Script*, it is referred to as "Merit inscription in honor of Guiyang prefect Zhou Jing."

"Treatise" (*Hequshu*) with an emphasis on the sentence, "Governor Li Bing cut through Mount Lidui and prevented the harm of the violent water" despite some differences elsewhere. We may understand it as the later generations' effort to interpret the *Records* rather than quoting different versions of it, like the way that "Treatise" (*Hequshu*) quotes *The Book of Xia* that uses terms more accessible to its contemporary readers to replace the originals. The "violent water"—*pushui*— as interpreted in *Explaining Simple and Analyzing Compound Characters*, in the chapter "Water," means "heavy rain. Sometimes called *mo*." The flood after heavy rain is thus called *pushui* or *moshui*. The *Gazetteer of Guan County*, in the chapter called "Waters," suggested, "Not a Mo River, other than the [Min] River." It means that the *moshui* in the "Treatise" (*Hequshu*) is not a river's name—the Dadu River that appears in the rest of the *Records* and the *Book of Han*. In addition, the fact that both "Treatise" (*Hequshu* and *Gouxuzhi*) focus on the Min River refutes the explanation of *moshui* as a river in these two chapters.

Lidui—Mount Min

At the end of "Treatise on Rivers and Waterways" (*Hequshu*), Sima Qian wrote:

> "I have ascended Mount Lu from the south and seen the nine rivers that Yu had tamed. I have also been to Taihuang at Kuaiji, climbed Mount Gusu, and watched the five lakes. I have traveled to the east and seen Luorui, Dapei, and Yinghe and rode along the rivers of Huai, Si, Ji, Lei, and Luo. I have also traveled to Mount Min and Lidui to the west and Shuofang to the north. I must say that the benefits and damages that waters bring can be equally significant!"

Here, the name Lidui is mentioned again with a more accurate location in the State of Shu in western China. *Zhui* is the "ancient form of *dui*," cited Pei Yin in *The Collected Commentaries to the Records of the Grand Historian*. Liu Yuan (1768—1855) explains that "the foot of the mountain is separate on the other side as if not related to Mount [Min]. Thus, it is called *lidui* (detached hill)." More specifically, it is an individual mountain separated from Mount Yulei in Dujiangyan City today. Before Li Bing excavated Mount Yulei, Mount Lidui was its root. People used to think of Mount Min as an enormous mountain chain stretching several hundred miles from County Min in Gansu to Mount

Qingcheng in Sichuan, and Mount Yulei was part of it. The "Mount Min" that Sima Qian referred to is the section of the mountain chain in Sichuan.

There are multiple ways that Lidui is recorded in ancient texts, three from the Han Dynasty alone. One from "Treatise on Rivers and Waterways" (*Hequshu*) in *Records of the Grand Historian*, another from "Treatise on Rivers and Canals" (*Gouxuzhi*), and the third from *Ode to Governor Zhou of Guiyang*. Although their writings are different, the pronunciation is the same. Perhaps, *lidui* was originally vocabulary from the ancient Shu dialect, meaning huge rocks or isles in rivers detached from the main bodies of the mountains, and it was transliterated into different Han characters at different times. There are more than forty *liduis* in the Ba Shu regions, mostly created by rivers or other natural forces. The only artificial *lidui*—and the most popular one—is Dujiangyan. The second most famous one is now known as Mount Wuyou, near the Leshan Giant Buddha.

The Stone Rhinoceroses—Heaven-Connecting Rhinoceros Horn

Another outstanding achievement of Li Bing, with a profound legacy other than the excavation of Lidui, was the five stone rhinoceroses he built in response to the flood. "Two were placed in his residence, one under the market bridge, and two in the river to tame the water spirit. The place was later named after the stone rhino."

This was a sorcery practice that Du Fu referred to as *yasheng* in *The Poem of the Stone Rhinoceros*. Quoting *Guangya*, Sima Zhen stated that "*ya* means repress." Thus, *yasheng* means "repressing and defeating" people, objects, or demons through sorcery or prayer. The traditions of putting up New Year couplets or mug wood at the Dragon Boat Festival that still prevail today also derived from *yasheng* practices.

The stone rhinoceroses were modeled after some species of rhinos. The question is, why?

In the first volume of *The State of Chu, Strategies of the Warring States* is written:

> To break the alliance of the other warring states in the east, the Qin
> minister Zhang Yi visited the King of Chu and said, "Qin has half of the
> world's land, and its terrain conditions are favorable, with mountains and

rivers to protect its borders. It also has the world's most powerful army, with millions of brave soldiers, thousands of war chariots, and tens of thousands of cavalrymen. The provisions are plentiful, and the laws are established, so the soldiers are ready and willing to die in wars. Our ruler is strict and wise, and our commanders are experienced and fearless. If we dispatch our troops, we can easily seize critical points such as Mount Chang and cut your alliance in two. By that time, whoever refuses to surrender will be destroyed first ... the States of Ba and Shu to the west of Qin are about three thousand *li* from the Chu capital by water. [If the Qin troops attack the Chu from the waterway,] ships containing fifty people and provisions for three months can travel three hundred *li* per day and arrive at Hanguan within ten days. If Hanguan is lost, then everywhere to the east of Jingling, including Qianzhong and Wujun, will no longer be yours...."

The King of Chu said, "My country is remote and isolated on the east sea, and I am young and ignorant of ruling a country. Thanks to your teaching, I am enlightened and shall respectfully follow onward on behalf of my country." He thus sent an envoy with a hundred chariots to present a *jihai* rhinoceros horn and a night-luminescent jade *bi* to the King of Qin.

"The *jihai* rhinoceros horn should be *haiji* rhinoceros horn," commented Wang Niansun, also called the "heaven-connecting rhinoceros horn." According to the "Inner Chapter" of the *Baopuzi*,

> Get an authentic heaven-connecting rhinoceros horn above two inches and carve it into the shape of a fish. When a person carries it in his mouth and goes in the water, it will give way to him. When he is three feet deep in the water, he can breathe. Get a heaven-connecting rhinoceros horn with red lines like threads from the head to tail, fill it with rice, and put it among the chickens. The chickens will try to eat the rice, but they will get frightened and retreat before they can be several inches near it. Therefore, the southerners call it the heaven-connecting rhinoceros or *haiji* (chicken-frightening) rhinoceros horn. Put this type of horn on barnyards, and birds dare not gather around them. Please put it in the courtyard on dense foggy nights so it does not get wet from the moisture.
>
> Rhinos with this type of horn shine brightly like torches in deep mountains at dim dusks. Stir the horn in poison, and it will generate white

foams and get detoxified. Stir it in non-toxic drinks, and there will be no foam. Therefore, when traveling in foreign places with venomous insects, it is often [recommended] that one stirs the food and drinks with the horn whenever dining outside. If a poisoned arrow attacks one, stick the horn in his wound, and he shall be cured when foam comes out. Heaven-connecting rhinoceros horns can be an antidote because these rhinos only eat poisonous and thorny plants, but never soft and smooth ones. When they are one year old, their horns will fall off. If people can capture them during this time, they may replace their horns with fake ones carved in the shape of the horn, and the animals will not know the difference. The following year, they will again [grow out new horns and] replace them [thinking it is their first time doing so]. Other rhinoceros horns can also detoxify poisons but are less efficient than heaven-connecting ones.

The "haiji rhinoceros horns" that the King of Chu presented to the King of Qin as a symbol of submission were possibly an "authentic heaven-connecting horn." Aside from its magical powers in exorcism and detoxification, the way it can part water was probably the most impressive to people for the longest time, as recorded in the Ming Dynasty novel *The Plum in the Golden Vase*.

> Even the great lord of Dongjing, who has jade and golden belts, doesn't have this rhino horn belt. This one is a water rhino horn, not a terrestrial one. You'll see, get a bowl of water and put it gently in, the water will be parted to the sides. This thing is priceless. Also, it can light up thousands of miles for a whole night.

In chapter twenty-four of the *Water Margin*, old Mrs. Wang praises the wealth of Ximen Qing for having "the horns on rhinos' heads and the tusks in elephants' mouths." The "heaven-connecting horns" may be called water rhino horns because of their ability to part water. The Tang poet, Bai Juyi, mentioned these horns and their handicrafts multiple times in his works. For example, "belt adorned by the heaven-connecting horn" from "Three poems on random thoughts," "Taming rhino, taming rhino, the heaven-connecting rhino has the frightening torso and look but the [magical] 'chicken-frightening' horns" from "Taming rhino, regretting the difficulty of serving in politics to the end," and "white, heaven-connecting horn belt" from "Writing to Minister Pei in the North."

The ancient land of Shu, especially the Mount Min area, was rich with rhinos. The *Classic of Mountains and Seas* records, "The river comes out from Mount Min three hundred *li* to the northeast and enters the ocean. There were many tortoises and crocodiles in the river and a lot of gold and jade in the mountains ashore. The vegetation was mostly plum blossoms and Chinese crabapple. Rhinoceroses, elephants, the legendary *kuiniu*, and golden pheasants were abundant." In many sources, the rhinoceros horns refer specifically to the heaven-connecting horns.

Following the rules of homeopathic magic, stone rhinos possess the same water-parting power as the real heaven-connecting rhinos do. As Frazer indicates in "Sympathetic magic," *The Golden Bough*, "If ordinary stones are considered to have general magical effects because of their weight and hardness, then special stones are considered having special magical effects because of their special shape or color." The stone rhinos were this kind of "special stone," and the "special magical effects" they possess is preventing the harm of floods. In mythical terms, their purpose is thus described as "to tame the water spirit," or "water demon" in "Rhapsody of Shu Capital."

Stone Oxen—Stone Worship and Rhino Worship

Li Bing was one of many who made stone rhinoceroses. In the *Biographies of the Kings of Shu*, it is recorded: "The fifth-generation ruler since the King of Kaiming, Kaiming Shang, discarded the title of King and reclaimed the title of Lord. God sent him five giants who could move Mount Shu away. When the King died, the five giants established a giant rock thirty *zhang* tall weighing thousands of tons (to commemorate them). It was called 'stone bull.' Even tens of thousands of men could not push it."

> The Lord of Shu owned the land of Ba and Shu. He originally lived in Fanxiang, Guangdu, and then moved to Chengdu. King Hui of Qin sent Zhang Yi and Sima Cuo to annex Shu and made Chengdu a city of Qin. The city government of Chengdu was originally at Chili Street. Still, Zhang Ruo moved it to the inner city and built governmental offices and receptions in the same structures as those in Chang'an.
>
> At first, the Lord of Shu refused to submit to King Hui of Qin, and the latter could not reach the land. [Once, when] the Lord of Shu was hunting at Baogu with tens of thousands of followers, he suddenly ran into King

Hui of Qin. The King of Qin gave the lord a basket of gold, and the lord also rewarded him with presents in return. [Later,] the presents changed into dirt and clay, and King Hui was furious. His ministers, however, bowed twice and congratulated him, "Dirt is earth. It means that Your Majesty will definitely obtain the land of Shu."

The Chronicle of King Hui of Qin records, "King Hui of Qin wanted to attack Shu, so he made five stone bulls and put gold behind them. When the Shu people saw it, they thought the bulls could produce gold. When they saw the grooms with the bulls, they thought that these were heavenly creatures. The Lord of Shu believed them, sending several thousand men and the five giants to bring the stone bulls back to Shu. Three of them were brought to Shu, and the dragging created a path behind them. Thus, the King of Qin gained access to Shul and sent prime minister Zhang Yi [to lead the army] to attack Shu via the stone-bull path."

The "heavenly bull" easily reminds us of heaven-connecting rhinos, and we can see that the tradition of stone-bull worship could be traced back to ancient Shu long ago. The usage of stone bulls and stone rhinos are sometimes interchangeable, such as in *Imperial Encyclopedia*, Volume 51, which states, quoting *Gazetteer of Jiangxi*, "The legendary deity is named Li Bing, who was the Governor of Shu during Duke Xiao of Qin's reign. He made five *stone bulls* to tame the water demon." King Hui and Li Bing, who built the stone bulls and stone rhinos, took advantage of the Shu people's worship of rocks and rhinos to achieve their military and constructional purposes. The two kinds of prayer are elaborated in *Chronicles of Huayang*,

> The ninth King of Kaiming established the temple of the ruling house. He referred to wine as *li* and music as *jing*. He made red a venerated color and changed the title King to Lord. At that time, five giants in Shu could move mountains and lift tons of weight. Whenever the ruler of Shu died, they put giant rocks over thirty inches and thousands of tons to commemorate him. These rocks formed a forest now called *sunli*. The rulers did not have posthumous titles and were known as the green, red, black, yellow, and white kings. After King Kaiming dreamed about moving out of the city, he relocated the capital to Chengdu.

During King Xian of Zhou's reign, the Lord of Shu owned the land of Bao and Han. The lord met King Hui of Qin while hunting in the valley. King Hui gave him a basket of gold, and he returned with valuable gifts. [However,] the gifts changed into the dirt, and King Hui was furious. His ministers congratulated him and said, "Heaven adores Qin, and Your Majesty shall gain the land of Shu." King Hui was pleased. He made five stone bulls and put gold behind them, saying that these "bulls could produce gold." He also ordered several hundred grooms to "attend to" the bulls. The Shu people were delighted when they heard about the bulls and requested to have them. King Hui gave his consent. So, the Lord of Shu sent the five giants to bring the bulls back. But when he discovered they did not produce any gold, he became angry and asked to return them, mocking the Qin people as "calf shepherds of the east." The King of Qin laughed at him and said, "I may be grazing calves, but I will obtain Shu."

There was a man—a mountain spirit—in Wudu who changed into a beautiful woman. The Lord of Shu made her his wife. But the empress was not used to the new environment and wanted to leave. The Lord begged her to stay and wrote "Dongping's Song" to entertain her. [Nevertheless,] the empress died soon afterward. The lord missed her in sorrow and ordered the five giants to build a tomb for the empress with soil from Wudu. The tomb was as high as dozens of inches tall, with a stone mirror on top. It is now Mount Wudan in the north of Chengdu. The heartbroken lord later wrote "Song of Yeyu" and "Song of Guilong" for her. He also buried these tomb makers [after they died] and commemorated them with giant rocks. There was a massive rock in Chengdu with a perimeter of about six inches and a height of thirty inches. There was another similar giant rock at Pi Bridge, about eighteen miles from the city. Old people said these giant rocks were brought here by the five giants. During Gongsun Shu's time, the Wudan rock broke apart, and Secretary Ren Wengong signed, "Alas, the wise man of the west had died, and I may as well." He passed away in the middle of the year.

In the thirty-second year of King Xian of Zhou's reign, [the Lord of] Shu sent an envoy to pay respect to Qin. This was because the King Hui of Qin often sent beautiful women to Shu, and the Lord of Shu was touched. King Hui knew Lord Shu's lecherous nature and sent five [Qin] women to marry him. The Lord ordered the five giants to welcome them. When they arrived at Zitong, they saw a giant snake crawling into a cave. One of them pulled onto its tail but was no match for its strength. The others came to help, shouting when the mountain collapsed. The five giants were killed on the spot, and so were the five women. The mountain split into five with a stone plate on top of the peak. Wretched, the Lord of Shu mounted it, named the mountains "Five Ladies' Tomb Mountains," and built a terrace to commemorate his empress. The mountains today are called "Five Giants Tomb Mountains."

The story described in the last paragraph inspired Li Bai for his famous poem, "Under the crumbled peak the five brave warriors died, then the ladder to heaven hooked the stone-wood bridge's side." The "five giants" or "five warriors" might have been five imperial stone crafters of the Lord of Shu, and that's why all the ruins of giant rocks are related to them,[3] proving again the widespread and deep-rooted stone worship in ancient Shu by their abundance.

The Name of the Former *Fujun* Li of the Shu State Was Bing— the Three Stone Figures—Taming the Water

In 1974, Bridge Anlan was moved due to the construction of a water gate for the Dujiangyan Project. On March 3, a three-meter-tall stone statue of Li Bing, built in 168, was excavated from the riverbed under the No. 3 abutment. There was a line of inscription in *li* characters on the figure's shirt that read, "the name of the former *fujun* Li was Bing," and two other lines on each of his sleeves that read,

> On the twenty-fifth day of the lunar month, the first year of Jianning, ministers of water supervision

Yin Longchang and Chen Yi built three divine stone figures to tame the water forever.

Some modern scholars thought the term *fujun* was an honorific appellation for deities or for state governors in the Qin and Han dynasties. Neither of these two arguments is accurate. In comparison, Gu Yanwu's discussion of the term "the state governor of the Han Dynasty" in Volume 24, *Records of Daily Gains in*

---

3. See *Detailed Explanation of the Five Heroes* by Wu Jingheng.

Knowledge, sounds more plausible, and here are two reasons.

"The stele of the late palace garrison, *fujun* Heng of Han," contemporary to the statue, begins with the sentence "the name of *fujun* is Fang," with the identical structure seen previously. Heng Fang, who had served multiple posts as Governor of Beiping, Governor of Yingchuan, and palace garrison, was revered as *fujun* in the same way as Fan Min, the Governor of Ba, in "The Stele of the Former Governor of Ba, *fujun* Fan of Han." In the *Epilogue of Immortal Tang Gongfang*, Volume 8 of *Exposition of Zhouqing*, Sun Yirang said,

> Lord Tang was from Chenggu (Chengdu?), which belongs to the Prefecture of Hanzhong indicated by the *Book of Han*. The stele states that "during the second year of Wang Mang's reign, Lord [Tang] was a government officer [of Hanzhong]." It also says, "The Governor's office was in the western city, about seven hundred *li* from his home. However, he could instantly appear whenever he was summoned, which shocked the entire staff. They spoke to the *fujun*, who made Tang a member in his office." The office was the Governor's office, and *fujun* was the Governor.

In the *Book of the Later Han*, we see the appellation of *fujun* connected with the names of Ruan Kuang—Governor of Nanyang, Bao Yu—Governor of Nan, Chen Deng—Governor of Guangling, and Zhang Xi—Governor of Yuesui. In addition, the Governor of Lujiang in the poem "Southeast Fly the Peacocks" as well as the Governor of Yuzhang in "Moral and Virtue," *A New Account of the Tales of the World*, are also referred to as *fujun*. As soon as the state governor Chen Fan, "Arrived at his post, he immediately asked where Xu Ruzi was and wished to meet him first. His secretary said, 'the people would like their *fujun* to enter his office first.'"

Based on the evidence above, we can thus know that "*fujun* Li" was the honorific title Li Bing had earned in the Eastern Han Dynasty.

The detailed inscriptions on the statue indicate that it was the most distinguished among the "three divine stone figures" that Yin Longchang and Chen Yi built. The other two statues were probably Li Bing's subordinates. One featuring a figure with a shovel was found in 1975, about 37 meters from Li Bing's statue. It was smaller and fragmentary, with only simple inscriptions such as a title and name or no inscription.

The construction of stone figures didn't start in the Eastern Han Dynasty.

"Chronicles of Shu," *Chronicles of Huayang* records that Li Bing "made three stone figures in the three rivers. The river gods promised him that the water would not be lower than their ankles during dry seasons and would not be over their shoulders during wet seasons." By the Eastern Han Dynasty, Li's figures had probably already been destroyed, so Yin and Chen decided to rebuild them. It is also likely that there was more than one reconstruction because a total of five statues had been found up to 2014.

What was the need to build the three stone figures?

According to the inscription, the purpose of these figures was to "tame the water."[4] In other words, these figures served the same function as the five stone rhinoceroses.

Let the Water Flow by Itself—Beijiangbeng—*Yan*

Like "Treatise on Rivers and Waterways" (*Hequshu*), *Argument of Politics* written by Cui Shi acknowledged Li Bing's contribution by saying, "Li Bing from the prefecture of Shu dug through Mount Lidui and brought in the two rivers. Yizhou still relies on them today."

Cai Yong's *Eulogy of Fanhui Canal of Jingzhao* points out the significance of these ancient water conservancy projects,

> The wise and insightful gentlemen established agriculture. They took advantage of the terrain conditions and let the water flow by itself. The land and its people thus forever benefit from the water. When it comes to Ximen [bao]'s merit in Ye, Zheng Guo's in Qin, and Li Bing's in Shu, these were the ways of having trusted ministers to rule.

The concept of "dam" (*yan* 堰, written as 鄢) was applied in the "Stele of the late Governors Guo Ze and Zhao Si" from 199. At that time, Dujiangyan was locally referred to as Beijiangbeng. Given that the Shu people used the word *beng* 埄 (also written as 堋) to refer to dams, the term *beng yan* 埄鄢 is also mentioned in the stele inscription for Dujiangyan.

---

4. The word for "tame," *mi* 珎, was later written as *zhen* 珍 and read as *zhen* 镇. According to Du Zichun and *Zihuibu*, "*zhen* 珍 is the same as *zhen* 镇."

King Zhao of Qin Appointed Li Bing the Governor of Shu—King Xiaowen of Qin Appointed Li Bing the Governor of Shu

"King Zhao of Qin appointed Li Bing the Governor of Shu. [Li Bing] dredged two rivers in Chengdu and irrigated tens of thousands of acres of fields. When the [river] god demanded two women to be his wives, Bing sent his daughters to the temple. He made a toast to the god, but the wine cup remained still. He thus harshly scolded [the river god] and suddenly disappeared. After some time, two black bulls were seen fighting on the riverbank. Later, [Li Bing] returned and addressed his followers, panting and sweating, 'I'm exhausted from fighting, won't you help me? The one facing south with white on its waist is me.' His secretary thus struck the bull facing north, and the river god died."[5]

The author of *Comprehensive Meaning of Customs and Mores* was also a Governor of Taishan in the Eastern Han Dynasty. He was the first to suggest that Li Bing served in this position approximately during King Zhao of Qin's reign, between 306 to 251 BCE. Some scholars believe that the time of Li Bing's appointment was in accordance with Zhang Ruo's assumption of the post of State Governor of Qianzhong in the 30th year of King Zhao. Therefore, Li probably ruled Shu under Qin sometime between 277–238 BCE. However, there is no proof that Li was the only Governor between Zhang Ruo and Governor Jin, and *Comprehensive Meaning's* assertion about Li Bing's service is also not exclusive. According to *Chronicles of Huayang*, "After the Zhou Dynasty ended, King Xiaowen of Qin appointed Li Bing the Governor of Shu." With the records in the Qin bamboo slips *Chronicles*, some scholars thus indicate that Li Bing was Governor of Shu between 251 and 250 BCE during King Xiaowen's reign.

Li Bing in the Form of a Bull—the River God in the Form of a Bull

Commentary on the Water Classic was the earliest source to include the fight between Li Bing and the river god. Quoting *Comprehensive Meaning of Customs*

---

5. See *Comprehensive Meaning of Customs and Mores* quoted by Zhang Shoujie in the *Legitimate Annotations to the Records of the Grand Historian.*

and Mores,

> King Zhao of Qin appointed Li Bing as the Governor of Shu. [Li Bing]
> dredged two rivers in Chengdu and irrigated tens of thousands of acres of
> fields. Every year, the [river] god demanded two virgins to be his wives, so
> Bing sent his own daughters to the temple. There, he made a toast to the
> god, but the wine cup remained still. He thus harshly scolded [the river
> god] and suddenly disappeared. After a long time, two bulls were seen
> fighting on the riverbank. Later, [Li Bing] returned. Sweating, he said to his
> followers, 'I'm exhausted from fighting. You must help me. The one facing
> south with white on its waist is me.' His secretary thus struck the bull facing
> north, and the river god died. The people of Shu admired his spirit, and all
> robust young men were named "Bing'er" after him.

The apotheosis of the river was first seen in the Western Han Dynasty.
Rhapsody of the Shu Capital recorded it as *shui chi*, water dragon. Explanations of
chi as an animal are provided by various writers, including Sima Xiangru, Wen
Ying, Zhang Yi, Xu Shen, Lu Qiu, and Wang Hui.

In the Eastern Han Dynasty, probably influenced by oral creation in the Shu
area, the river god changed from a dragon to a bull and fought with Li Bing,
who also transformed into a bull. According to the *Legitimate Annotation to the
Records of the Grand Historian*, the bulls were black, so there was a chance that
they were rhinos. In *Chronicles of the King of Shu*, Li Bing was a human and made
stone rhinos to tame the water demon. In the *Comprehensive Meaning of Customs
and Mores*, he had become a god and could fight the river demon in the form of
a rhino. The water demon represents the flood, and so *Notes of Beitang* records,
"After Bing killed the river god, people no longer suffered from droughts or
floods." By this time, Li Bing was both a man and a god in people's eyes.

The First Temple for Li Bing

Notes of Beitang records, "King Zhao of Qin adopted Tian Gui's advice and
appointed Li Bing the Governor of Shu. He dredged the two rivers and irrigated
tens of thousands of acres of land. Qin Shi Huang, who benefited from his merit,
annexed all states and established a temple for Li Bing." In another volume in
the same book, however, it quotes, "King Zhao of Qin adopted Tian Guang's

advice and attacked Shu. Later, he appointed Li Bing as the Governor of Shu. Li dredged the two rivers and irrigated tens of thousands of acres of land. However, the water demon constantly harmed the people of Shu. Li thus killed the demon, and people no longer suffered from droughts or floods."

Presumably, Tian Gui and Tian Guang were the same people, the *bole* of Li Bing and the benefactor of all people of Shu. The dredging of two rivers meant the preliminary construction of Dujiangyan, which was already introducing significant and long-lasting benefits for common people as well as for state rulers. This was why Qin Shi Huang built a shrine for Li Bing, which was the construction foundation for the River Lord's Temple and Two Kings Temple in later generations. This temple undoubtedly accelerated the procedure of Li Bing's apotheosis.

Did Li Bing have a title in the Han Dynasty?

Li Bing was revered as a god by the Later Han period, and it seems reasonable for him to have an honorific title granted by the ruler of the time. According to the "Joint biography of the three river gods," "Li Bing received the title of 'Lord Zhaoying' from Emperor Gaozu of Han and then that of 'King Da'an' in the Later Han Dynasty." Yet in *The Song Government Manuscript Compendium*, the title of "Lord Zhaoying" is suggested to be Li Bing's son, "Li Bing's eldest son, Lord Zhaoying Lingxian was granted the title of Lord Zhaoying Lingxian Xuanhui the second year of Chunxi (1175)."

Rivers and Canals Spread Like Veins in the Six Dynasties

Mount Guanban—the Golden Dam

The first imperial ruler who inspected Dujiangyan was Liu Shan, the last emperor of Shu Han during the Three Kingdoms Period. "The summer of the fourteenth year of Jianxing (236), the emperor arrived in the County of Jian, mounted Mount Guanban, and watched the Wen River flow."[6] Mount Guanban was Mount Lidui. As *Commentary on the Water Classic* noted, "the Governor of Shu, Li Bing, built a

---

6. See "Biology of the Last Emperor," *Records of the Three Kingdoms.*

great dam called *Jianbeng*, also called *Jianyan*. Mount Guanban is above it."

The Western Jin author, Zuo Si, spent considerable time collecting materials about Shu and composed the *Rhapsody of the Shu Capital*. In it, he said,

> The foundation of the capital of Shu was probably established in ancient times, and the state formed in the Middle Ages ... two rivers flow across the land, and the high mountains of Emei guarded its border ... peacocks fly in flocks, and rhinos and elephants run with each other side by side ... Rich water comes from Mount Min on the west ... rivers, and canals spread like veins across the land. The millet was bright and shiny, and the rice was thick and full ... Every home has a well of mineral spring, and every household has a garden with mandarin and pomegranate ... the state's territory stretches across Jindi on the west and Yujin on the east.

Li Bing's Achievements—Projects Other Than Jianyan

Two writers from Shu are particularly important in the history of Dujiangyan, Yang Xiong and Chang Qu, whose works were briefly introduced in the previous chapter. We will now look specifically at *Chronicles of Shu*'s description of Li Bing.

> After the Zhou Dynasty ended, King Xiaowen of Qin appointed Li Bing the Governor of Shu.
>
> Bing was an expert in astrology and geography. When he arrived at Jiandi County, it was believed that he encountered gods when he saw two mountain peaks facing each other like gate pillars. He thus built three shrines in the water and presented sacrifices with livestock and jades. In the Han Dynasty, [the emperor] sent envoys several times to worship them.
>
> Bing built a dam across the River Pi and River Jian to divide a tributary for shipping in the state. Mount Min was richly covered with call tapas, cypress, and bamboo. When they broke and fell, they were sent down by the river so that the people could quickly obtain abundant timber. The water nourished the soil and cultivated thousands of miles of paddy fields. Farmers could bring in water for irrigation during the dry seasons, and during rainy seasons, they could shut the water gate to prevent floods. "People could control the flood and drought and never suffer from famine. [The State of Shu] was thus known by the world as 'the Heavenly State.'"

[Li Bing] also made five stone rhinos to tame the water demon and placed them at Xiniuli. Later, two of them were relocated to the market bridge and the river.

He made three stone figures standing in the water at Baishayou and had the water god promise to "not let the water run lower than their ankles during dry seasons and not higher than their shoulders during rainy seasons."

At that time, the water of River Mo was fast and dangerous at the Hunya cliff, and it had threatened the safety of ships passing by for generations. Li Bing thus ordered soldiers to cut the Hun cliff and let the water flow smoothly. Some said that the water god was angry about Li Bing's action, so Li Bing fought the god with a knife [and won]. His legacy was still beneficiary to people today.

In Bodao County, where the cliff was too rugged and steep to cut, [Li Bing ordered to] gather firewood and burn the rocks, leaving colorful stains of red and white. He also dredged the river Wenjiang that went across Lintong ... River Lu that went across Shifang ... and River Mian that went across Mianzhu ... which irrigated the corps along their way. This was why the People of Shu called the soils of Pi and Fan "fat" and that of Mian and Luo "fertile."

He built seven bridges over the two rivers in the southwest—Chong Bridge, Market Bridge, Jiang Bridge, Wanli Bridge, Yili Bridge (or Ze Bridge), Changsheng Bridge, and Yongping Bridge. The old people said, "Li Bing built seven bridges by the seven stars in heaven."

The story of Li Bing "encountering gods" at Min River was first recorded in the *Chronicles of the King of Shu*. The sacrifices of *chen* (sink) referred to the ritual of sinking livestock into the river when praying for peace from the river god prevalent during the Shang and Zhou dynasties and still visible today at Dujiangyan during *fangshui* holiday.

To dig the cliffs, the ancient workers gathered firewood to burn the rocks, poured water on them to create cracks, and then cut with iron tools.[7] In April

---

7. Liquid cast iron was produced during the Spring and Autumn Periods. See "Yigutie," *The Commentary of Zuo, Production, Manufacture and Management of Iron Farm Tools in the Qin Dynasty* by Chen Hong, Chapter 1, and page 232 of *The History of Iron Smelting Technology in*

1955, Guo Moruo visited Dujiangyan and wrote, after careful survey and research, "Li Bing, who dug through Mount Lidui and built mineral water wells, was indeed an engineering technologist from two thousand years ago. Some thought Mount Lidui was Mount Wuyou at Jiazhou. I am from Jiazhou, and today I see the remaining marks of cutting [on the cliffs] at Baopingkou; thus, I know the saying of [Mount Lidui at] Jiazhou is wrong."

The Two Rivers—the Two *Records of Yizhou*

Ren Yu, a Shu writer from the State of Song in the Southern Dynasty, said in *Records of Yizhou*, "the two rivers referred to River Pi and River Liu." River Pi (River Pei or River Jian) is today's Baitiao River, and River Liu (or River Jian) is the Zouma River.

In *Description Encompassing the Earth*, quoted in *The Proper Explanation of the Records of the Grand Historian*, "the great river flowing northeast is also called River Wen, Guanqiao River, River Qing, and River Shui. River Pi flowing southeast is also called Chengdu River, Shiqiao River, Zhongri River, and River Nei."

Contemporary to Ren Yu, Li Ying, who had served as governmental secretary of Yizhou, had also written *Records of Yizhou* that said, "there was a stone bull at the north of the city made by Li Bing ... Guankou, seven miles west of Qingshuilu, was called Heaven's Gate in the past because two standing rocks looked like gate pillars."

Jianbeng—Du'anyan—the "Dam Officers"

The *Chronicles of Huayang* left a profound influence on later generation writings, especially reflected in the *Commentary on the Water Classic* by Li Daoyuan,

---

Ancient China by Yang Kuan, page 49 of *Illustration of Material and Cultural Materials in the Han Dynasty* by Sun Ji, page 153 of *Eight Hundred Years of Yan State* by Peng Hua. For the popular use of iron materials in the Warring States period, see *About Leigudun Tombs* by Zhang Changping, *The Production Tool Casting Model of the Warring States Period found in Rehe Xinglong* by Zheng Shaozong, Chapter 5 of *History of Iron Smelting Technology in Ancient China*, page 656 of *The Ancient Kingdom of Shandong and Surnames* by Pang Zhengao, pages 146–148 and 154–156 of *Eight Hundred Years of Yan State*, pages 33–40 of *A History of Chinese Chemistry* by Zhang Zigao, and pages 39–40 of *A History of Science and Technology* by Wang Yucang.

King Zhao of Qin appointed Li Bing the Governor of Shu. Li Bing saw two mountains standing like gate pillars at Didao County and called them Heaven's Gate.

The River Wen comes from Mount Min, flows south and then east, and joins the great river.

The river flows through Du'an County, where you can find the Taoguan Pass and Emperor Wu of Han's temple. Li Bing built the great dam Jianbeng here with a left and right opening. The river joined River Pi and Jian for shipping. [Ren Yu's] *Records of Yizhou* states, "when the river arrives at Du'an ... its mainstream flows east, bringing down broken bamboo and trees from the mountain with it and irrigating multiple provinces." Li Bing made three stone figures standing in the water at Baishayou and made the river god promise "not to have the water run lower below their ankles during dry seasons and not above their shoulders during rainy seasons." Therefore, it was said that "People could control the flood and drought and never suffered from famine. [The State of Shu] was thus known by the world as 'the Heavenly State.'" The dam was commonly known as the "great dam of Du'an," the dam of Jian, or the Golden Dam.

During his northern expedition, Zhuge Liang summoned a thousand and two hundred people to guard the dam with the support of state funding and appointed dam officers.

Li Bing knew the water system well and built mineral water wells across the province. He cut open the mountains and let the water flow through, forming lakes that nourished the land.

Li Bing built seven bridges along the rivers under the seven stars in the sky.

Li Bing guided the river to join the Wenjing River.

The river god created a vast lake with steep mountains that were impossible to cut. Li Bing thus gathered firewood to burn it [before digging]. Therefore, the cliffs are of different colors.

Chang Qu said, "Li Bing cut through mountains and dredged the River Luo that flows through Shifang County."

The establishment of the post "dam officer" did not start in the Three Kingdoms Period. The *dushuiyuan* mentioned in the inscription on Li Bing's statue and the *yuanshi* and *bengli* mentioned in the *Stele of the late Governors Guo Ze and Zhao Si* were all dam officers with a similar purpose.

Conclusion

Following *Commentary on the Water Classic*, *Universal Geography of the Taiping Era* said, "Du'anyan, built by Li Bing, was also called Jianyan. The Shu people called the dam *beng*." This dialect was further verified by the excavation of Guo Ze and Zhao Si's stele. *History of the Song Dynasty* states, "the Song army managed the Dujiangyan every year, controlling the river with cages filled with rocks to irrigate the fields." Here, *an* in Du'anyan is recorded as *jiang*, suggesting the name Dujiangyan was coined in the Northern Song Dynasty. Throughout history, Dujiangyan continued to nourish the Chengdu Plain and provide long-lasting benefits for all in China.

——— ✦◆✦ ———

CHAPTER 9

The "Three Stone Men" and the "Three Fairy Stone Men"

Since ancient times, there have been various rumors about stone men around Dujiangyan. In the *Records of Yizhou*, Li Ying, a native of Guanghan in the Southern Liang Dynasty, it is stated that "there were three stone men and five stone rhinoceroses to tame the water" at Dujiangyan. 厌 *yan* means 镇 *zhen* in Chinese. In the Eastern Han Dynasty, 厌水 *yanshui* was 珎水 *zhenshui*. It was mainly a form of sorcery, which Du Fu called "厌胜法 the method of aversion to victory." The term "厌胜" means "loathing and winning" and describes curses or prayers to suppress people, objects, or demons one hates. We now put up the couplets in Spring Festival and hang mugwort at Dragon Boat Festival. These were also originally aversions to the art of victory.

However, when and who did carve these three stone men?

The Stone Men of the Warring States That Were Lost and Nowhere to Be Found

It is said that Li Bing, the famous hero of water management, is the person who made the stone men. During the Eastern Jin Dynasty, Chang Qu, a native of Chongzhou, said in the *Chronicles of Huayang*, "Bing knew astronomy and geography, ... made three stone men at Baishayou under the Jade Lady Room, put them in the water, and made a deal with river god: 'Water exhaustion does not reach the foot. When there is much water, the water level does not exceed the shoulder.'" A little later, Li Daoyuan (466–527) described it more clearly in *Commentaries on the Water Classic*.

King Zhao of Qin appointed Li Bing as the Governor of Shu ... Bing went west at Baishayou under the Jade Lady Room, carved three stone men standing in the water, and inscribed the agreement with the river god on the stone men: "Water exhaustion does not reach the foot. When there is much water, the water level does not exceed the shoulder." Therefore, the Shu people can use it for irrigation when it is dry, and it does not block the water flow when it rains. That's why *Records of Yizhou* states: "Water and drought are at the people's disposal, famine is extinct, and there are thousands of miles of fertile fields, so the world is called Lu Hai, also known as Tian Fu. The postal pavilion is located on the weir." Baishayou is in the Dujiangyan upstream, situated in the present-day Baisha field of Dujiangyan City.

The inscription "Water exhaustion does not reach the foot. When there is much water, the water level does not exceed the shoulder" is engraved on the body of the stone man, roughly speaking: The feet of the stone man should not be exposed when the river is dry, and the shoulders of the stone man should not be exceeded when the river is rising. It is a mythical expression. To put it plainly, Li Bing set up the stone man, a Water Level Gauge, to monitor the Min River's water level and the water's size. It is very similar to the "Fuling Stone Fish," which measures the water level of the Yangtze River during dry periods. Can Chang Qu witness this stone man with nine inscriptions? I think it's impossible. Why? Because the three stone men had disappeared before the first year of the Jianning Reign (168 CE) in the Eastern Han Dynasty. Chang Qu should have relied on more reliable historical archives, such as the above-quoted "old records" and ancient books.

Stone Men of the Eastern Han Dynasty Unearthed One after Another

In 1974, the Dujiangyan hub project built the new outer river sluice; the original Anlan Bridge was moved down to the current location. On March 3, a stone statue of Li Bing was excavated in the riverbed under the Number Three outer river bridge base. The statue was built in the first year of the Jianning Reign (168) and is nearly three meters high. A clerical script is inscribed in the middle of its lapel, which can be read as "His Excellency Li Bing, Former Governor of Shu Prefecture."

On the left and fitting sleeves are inscriptions in clerical script, which can be read as "In the first year of the Jianning Reign, on the twenty-fifth day of the leap month, Yin Longchang and Chen Yi (Dushuiyuan), made three sacred stone figures of the three gods to tame the water thousands of years."

The stone statue of Li Bing was made by Yin Longchang and Chen Yi, both of whom imitated the "three stone figures." The official title of Yin Longchang and Chen Yi is Dushuiyuan which could be abbreviated as "Du Shui" and lower than the governor. As the most honored statue, Li Bing's stone statue has detailed inscriptions. The other two may be Li Bing's subordinate officials (such as *Zhubu*, an ancient official in charge of the paperwork under the chief official at all levels of the corps.), but the whereabouts of unknown.

On January 18, 1975, a more petite headless stone figure holding a shovel was unearthed 37 meters from where the stone statue of Li Bing was unearthed, later called the weir worker. This statue is now exhibited together with the figure of Li Bing in the Fulongguan of the Dujiangyan Scenic Area. There is reason to suspect that it is one of the "Three Fairy Stone Men."

On March 3, 2005, another headless stone statue of a man appeared during the construction of the Outer River Ropeway Bridge. It has been exactly 31 years since the date of the excavation of the stone statue of Li Bing. Is it also one of the "Three Fairy Stone Men"? We have not been excited for two days. On March 5, another headless stone statue was found near the No. One bridge abutment. On March 7, a diamond-shaped iron block, 20 cm long, 5 cm thick, weighing more than five kilos, was dug up on the annual maintenance site, just embedded in the stone statue base slot. The staff of the cultural relics department recognized at once that this is an ancient iron tenon connecting the ground mansion stone. But is it used to fix the base of the stone man? Or set the river bottom stone? Or is it embedded in the riverbank stones? Yet to be investigated.

Moreover, nine years later, another headless stone figure was found on April 24, 2014, when the excavator was working in the force reduction pool under the 7th and 8th holes of the outer river gate.

From 1974 to 2014, five stone figures were unearthed on four occasions within less than 100 meters of each other at the head of the Dujiangyan canal, all dressed in ancient Chinese robes and carved in the Han Dynasty. One of which can be identified as the statue of Li Bing due to an inscription (it can also be concluded that none of the five was carved during Li Bing's lifetime). The remaining four are all headless and inscriptionless and cannot be identified and later included in the list of "sacred stone figures" made in the Eastern Han Dynasty.

The Legacy of Chengdu Stone Figures after the Eastern Han Dynasty

After the Eastern Han Dynasty, the stone figures were inherited, and places other than Dujiangyan were learning from and emulating them. The *Chronicles of Huayang* in the Jiaqing Reign, Qing Dynasty records: "九里堤 Nine *Li* Dike: The ruling place is three 里 *li* to the east side of 洗瓦堰 Xiwa Weir. According to the last edition of *The General Chronicles*, the dikes were about three hundred 丈 *zhang* long, nine stone men and nine stone rhinos were placed, respectively, which were used by people in the past to control flooding. According to Wang Shixing's the *Record of Entering Shu*, "Chengdu used to flood frequently, so stone rhinoceroses were placed to tame the water. Ten stone rhinoceroses are in the east of the city, nine of which are placed by the river. This is probably what it means." The same book also describes, "Stone men and stone rhinos, used to manage the 万年堤 Wannian Dike outside the eastern city. There are nine stone men and nine stone rhinos each, which people probably used to control floods. Now only one stone rhino remains, and the rest are gone."

According to the *General Overview of Chengdu* written by Fu Chongju, we can know that 九里堤 Nine *Li* Dike is in Chengdu, while the 万年堤 Wannian Dike and 洗瓦堰 Xiwa Weir are in Huayang. Therefore, the statement "九里堤 Nine *Li* Dike: The ruling place is three 里 *li* to the east side of 洗瓦堰 Xiwa Weir" is wrong; it should be "万年堤 Wannian Dike: The ruling place is three 里 *li* to the east side of 洗瓦堰 Xiwa Weir." (The only "monuments to be verified" listed in the *General Overview of Chengdu* is "the stone man and stone rhino of Wannian Dike," and The *Chronicles of Unification of the Qing Dynasty* says "万年堤 Wannian Dike is on the east side of Huayang County, over 300 丈 *Zhang* long. Nine stone men and nine stone rhinos were placed to control floods," which is also proof.)

The fate of these nine stone men is the same as the "Three Stone Men" and the "Three Fairy Stone Men" in Dujiangyan, eventually all inevitable annihilation, and whether there is a chance to appear, we can wait and see.

The Three Stone Figures of Jintang in the Southern Song Dynasty

During the Southern Song Dynasty, there was a temple in Jintang where three stone statues were enshrined; perhaps it was the "Three Fairy Stone Men" belief after the Eastern Han Dynasty. Wang Xiangzhi's *Yu Di Ji Sheng* records: "Three Kings Beach is in Jintang Gorge, ten 里 *li* from Jintang County. All three kings have temples and stone statues, but no names are known. Some say that the three kings are Xia Yu, the god of Guankou, and King Cong." These three are all related to water management or Guankou (Dujiangyan), which can be significantly noted.

Inspired by this, we presume that the "Three Fairy Stone Men" in the Eastern Han Dynasty are Yu the Great, King Cong, and Li Bing, which does not seem too outrageous; the headless stone man holding a shovel is probably Yu the Great and not the weir worker.

CHAPTER 10

Research on the Inscriptions of the Three Stone Men during the Warring States Period

O n March 3, 1974, a round stone statue nearly three meters high was unearthed in Dujiangyan. A clerical script is inscribed in the middle of its lapel, which can be read as "His Excellency Li Bing, Former Governor of Shu Prefecture." On the left and fitting sleeves are inscriptions in clerical script, which can be read as "In the first year of the Jianning Reign, on the twenty-fifth day of the leap month, Yin Longchang and Chen Yi (Dushuiyuan), made three sacred stone figures of the three gods to tame the water thousands of years." Therefore, people call it the "Li Bing Stone Statue." The statue is so far above the natural person that it should be called "Li Bing's Divine Statue"—in addition to the self-identification of the "Divine Stone Man," stories contemporaneous with this statue also show that Li Bing had been deified by this time. For example, in his *Comprehensive Meaning of Customs and Mores*, Ying Shao (c. 153–196) wrote about Li Bing's transformation of a bull to kill the river god.

The stone statue with the inscription is one of the officials'"Three Fairy Stone Men" carved in the Eastern Han Dynasty, based on the "Three Stone Men" made by Li Bing, the Governor of Shu in the Warring States period, at Baishayou under the Jade Lady Room. One of the "Three Stone Men" should also be carved with inscriptions, just like the statue of Li Bing. The *Commentaries on the Water Classic* state that Li Bing "... made three stone figures, standing in the water, and carved to the gods of the river." This explains the inscription's existence. But what is the specific content of the description? There have been many different opinions, and it is hard to agree.

"Water exhaustion does not reach the foot. When there is much water, the water level does not exceed the shoulder." 【水竭不至足, 盛不没肩】Sources: Chang Qu (c. 291–361), *Chronicles of Huayang*, Volume 3, "Shu Zhi," Li Daoyuan, *Commentaries on the Water Classic*, Volume 3, "River Water," Lu Qiu, Preface of *Records of Chengdu*, Ye Tinggui, *Hailu Suishi*, Volume 3, "Stone Rhinoceros," *Jiuxiu Wanhuagu Qianji*, Volume 3, "Stone Rhinoceros."

Du Guangting (850–933), in *Congratulations to River God for Moving the Weir*, said this inscription as "涸脛泛肩之誓 *He Jing Fan Jian Zhi Shi*," (涸脛泛肩 is the summary of "Water exhaustion does not reach the foot. When there is much water, the water level does not exceed the shoulder." Even if not, we can at least deduce from this that the last word of the inscription Du saw was "shoulder.")

"There has been a pattern of water level abundance and retreat for many worship services since then. When the water is dry, the water level will not be lower than the foot; when the water is abundant, the water level will not be higher than the shoulder." 【俾后万祀, 水之盈缩, 竭不至足, 盛不没肩】Source: Huang Xiufu, *Maoting Kehua*, Volume 1, "Shu Wu Da Shui."

"When the water is dry, the water level will not be lower than the foot; when the water is abundant, the water level will not flood up to the waist." 【水竭不至足, 盛不没腰】Source: Ouyang Wen, *Yu Di Guang Ji*, Volume 30, "Chengdu Prefecture."

According to Yang Shen's *Jin Shi Gu Wen*, Volume 3, "The Oath of Li Bing, the Governor of Shu in Qin Dynasty, to the Gods of the River," it should say "竭不至足, 盛不没腰." There is a one-word difference in *Huangba Wen Ji*, Volume 12, "Oath of the River God Tablet," by Mei Dingzuo, which is "水竭不至足, 盛不没要."

"When the water is dry, the water level will not be lower than the foot; when the water is abundant, the water level will not be higher than the waist." 【水竭不至足, 盛不至腰】Source: Wang Xiangzhi, *Yu Di Ji Sheng*, Volume 151, "Chengdu Fulu · Yongkangjun · Jingwuxia." *Three Stone Men*, quoted in *Shu Ji*.[1]

---

1. The author of *Shu Ji* is unknown. Li Diaoyuan's *Supplement to the Shu Monuments* quotes Wang's *Yu Di Bei Mu*, which is "浅无至足, 深无至肩," but not in the present *Yu Di Bei Mu*.

"Later, when the water level is shallow, it will not be lower than the foot; when the water level is deep, it will not be higher than the shoulder."【后世浅无至足, 深无至肩】Source: Zhu Mu (?–1255), *Fang Yu Shen Lan*, Volume 54, "Pengzhou," cited *Ji Gu Lu*.[2]

"When the water level is dry, it will not go below the feet; when the water level rises, it will not flood to the shoulders."【涸不出足, 涨不至肩】Source: Zhao Daoyi, *Lishi Zhenxian Tidao Tongjian*, Volume 10, "Li Bing."

The above are stone inscriptions before the Yuan Dynasty, but the quotation by Chang Qu was the earliest and the most reliable.

The chapter of the *Big Weir* of *River Water* first cited the texts from *Records of Yizhou* by Ren Yu, then used the texts of *Shu Zhi*. The Ming scholars should have checked it. So, they thought these two paragraphs came from the same book, and the *Records of Yizhou* was written by Li Ying, not by Ren Yu. This mistake continued into the Qing Dynasty. As the quotation needs to be more precise and more followed, the inscriptions involved should not be credible, so that they can be ignored.

There were at least three other sayings in the Ming and Qing dynasties. They were written by Xu Rulong, Zhang Zhuo, and Peng Zunsi. They seem to be cited from the *Exhausting Overview of All Parts of the Empire*. These sayings are very late in the era, so adopting them is unnecessary.

---

2. This citation is not found in the present *Ji Gu Lu* nor the *Trek End* of *Ji Gu Lu*.

CHAPTER 11

———•◆•———

After the Stone Rhinoceros Sinks, the Waves Are at Rest

The historical facts and related remains of "Li Bing, Governor of Shu, made five stone rhinoceroses" have been recorded or witnessed from the time of Yang Xiong (53–18 BCE) until 1952. But only a few words are scattered in the sea of books, not forming a system. I have long paid attention to the search for materials in this area and sorted reference comparisons after several years of writing this article. Readers should read it carefully and then correct it. Then it will be worthy of my efforts.

Yang Xiong, a scholar of the Western Han Dynasty, wrote in the *Biographies of the Kings of Shu*: "When the river flooded with water, Li Bing, the Governor of Shu, made five stone rhinoceroses. Two were placed in the governor's residence, one under the market bridge and two in the water to tame the water monster. Therefore, the place was called Stone Rhinoceros Lane." *Imperial Reader of the Taiping Era*, Volume 890, cited the same sayings. But *Sibu Cong Kan* changed the place of one stone rhinoceros to the south of Chengdu.

Zhu Mu cited the same writing in *Gu Jin Shi Wen Lei Ju Hou Ji*, Volume 36, "Shu Zuo Shixi." *Guangbo Wuzhi* and *Yuding Yuan Jian Lei Han* all have the same record.

Eastern Jin scholar Chang Qu wrote in *Chronicles of Huayang*: "Li Bing made five stone rhinoceroses outside the city to control water monsters. The south of the river led to a stone rhinoceros' stream, which will be named this place as Rhinoceros Lane. Later two stone rhinoceroses were transferred: one was placed at Chengdu's Shiqiao Gate, today's Shi Niu Gate, and one was placed in the river. The city of Chengdu's southwest Shi Niu Gate is called Shi Qiao. Under the bridge is the river where the stone rhinoceroses lurk."

Li Ying, a scholar of the Southern Liang Dynasty, wrote in the *Records of Yizhou*: "There is a stone rhino on the north of Chengdu City, which Li Bing erected. The river water comes from Dujiangyan, and there are three stone men and five stone rhinoceroses to tame the water monster."

The Northern Wei scholar Li Daoyuan wrote in the *Commentary on the Water Classic*, Volume 33, "River Water": "At first, Zhang Yi was responsible for the construction of Chengdu City, the soil needed to build the city five kilos away from the city, digging the soil to form a large pit used to raise fish, is now the Wanqin pond. There is also the dragon dike pond on the north, east of the city has Qianqiu pond, west of the city has a willow pond, and northwest of the city has the Tianjing pond. Each small river is directly connected, winter and summer inexhaustible. Southwest of the two rivers has seven bridges. The West Gate on the Pi River is the Chongzhi Bridge; the market bridge is southwest of Shi Niu Gate. Wu Han entered Sichuan from Guangdu and ordered light cavalry to burn the market bridge first. Under the market bridge is the stone rhinoceros' abyss; Li Bing used to make five stone rhinoceroses, to tame the water monster. Diversion of water from the South River to form the stone rhinoceros canal; this area is the Rhinoceros Lane. Later transferred two stone rhinoceroses to the city, one on the market bridge, one sunk into the water."

Tang Dynasty scholar Lu Qiu wrote in the *Preface to Chengdu Records*, "Li Bing made five stone rhinoceroses to suppress the poisonous dragon; the order was rhinoceroses, which were later changed to two plow oxen."

Taiping Guangji, Volume 291, "Chengdu Records" mentioned: "After Li Bing killed the bull-shaped river god, the people of Shu were no longer harmed by the floods, and to this day, the big waves rushed to the temple of Li Bing, and they all retreated. So, the custom of bullfighting in Dujiangyan every spring and winter probably originated from this. Thousands of families live in the lowlands by the river south of the Li Bing Temple, and although they are relatively poor, they do not want to move away. Because there is a stone bull under the Li Bing temple."

The following is a poem by Du Fu, the great poet of the Tang Dynasty:

In heavy rains, one often finds rare green gems—

these things are a muddle and hard to explain clearly.

I suspect that in the olden days, these were tombs of a minister or grandee;

they set the stones up as markers and still survive today.

It is too bad that common ways love to obscure the truth;

it's also like lesser officials who flatter His Majesty.

Government by cultural influence is thrown in confusion;

the more extensive form is lost,

then one sees those who endanger the state receive generous grace.

Alas, you Stone Sprouts, commanding empty fame,

those who do not know better in later times will still come running here to look.

How can I get a bold man to cast them beyond the horizon,

to make people doubt no more, having seen what is behind it all?

Have you not seen how Shu's governor, in the time of Qin,

had stone carved and set up three rhinoceroses?

Since ancient times although there have been magic techniques to

suppress disasters,

Heaven produces the river waters that flow off to the east.

People of Shu boast that river flooding has not come near

Zhang Yi's Tower for over a thousand years.

This year Guankou Mountain has lost its population.

One might suspect that this event will embarrass the god.

Ultimately, we depend on dikes and levees

that come from collective effort,

piling wood and stone high to resist the autumn floods.

When the former kings laid down laws,

they always followed the right way;

how can weird mythical spirits be a part of human plans?

Alas, for you, three rhinos, you did not care for problems, eroding,

and losing pieces; you only go off with the long river.

If only one sees that the Primal Vapor is always in harmony,

one can naturally prevent the great waves from unleashing their depredations.

How can we find someone muscular to maintain Heaven's order?

—with our water and soil calm, the rhinos will flee and fade afar.

—Du Fu, The Stone Rhinoceroses: A Ballad

The following is a poem by Cen Shen, a poet of the Tang Dynasty:

> With the river's flood, waters did rise,
> Shu's people near became the fish's prize.
> Without the stone rhinoceros' blessed aid,
> Where would their cities stand, unafraid?
> Now the greatness of Governor Li we see,
> Surpassing Yu the Great, in victory.
>
> —CEN SHEN, *The Stone Rhinoceroses*

The following is a poem by Yong Tao, a poet of the Tang Dynasty:

> The troops of the enemies follow the willows of the Han.
> The barbarians pointed to the plums of the river.
> After the battle, I grieve for the blood.
> The burning of the remaining ashes.
> The stone rhinoceroses are not working.
> There is no more wine to remove the disaster.
>
> —YONG TAO, *Poem on Reflections after the Battle of Chengdu*

This poem was written in 829 CE after the Nanzhao attacked Chengdu. We can understand the rhinoceros in the text by referring to Du Fu's verse.

> Sometimes I go out from Green Chicken Ward
> and head to my thatched cottage on the western meadows.
> The public willows by Market Bridge have fine branches,
> And the wild plums on the River Road smell sweet.
> Going over to my bookcase,
> I arrange the scroll wrappers evenly,
> I inspect my medicine bag, checking the labels.
> No one realizes my comings and goings—
> this mood of careless laziness lasts so long!
>
> —DU FU, *The Western Suburban Fields*

According to *The General Records of Shu*, Li Bing made five stone rhinoceroses on the thirty-five *li* south of Chengdu: now a stone rhinoceros is in front of the Shengshou Temple in the southwest of Chengdu, and the temple has a dragon abyss, so the stone rhinoceros is used to control it; a stone rhinoceros is in the city of Records of Chengdunhua Bridge, the ancient market bridge. The dragon abyss is a well. Based on the records during the Kangxi period of the Qing Dynasty, the well was within the Great Hall of the temple. It was still preserved in the Republican period.

Li Jifu, a scholar of the Tang Dynasty, wrote in the *Chronicles of the Prefecture and County During the Yuanhe Reign*, Volume 32: "Xipu County, which was originally the boundary of Chengdu County, was separated from Chengdu County in the second year of the Chuigong Reign and set up as new county. In the past, Shu Governor Li Bing made five stone rhinoceros sunk in the water to control water monsters; this place is named because of this legend."

Yue Shi wrote in the *Universal Geography of the Taiping Era*, Volume 72: "Stone Rhinoceros:" Li Ying said: Li Bing set up the stone rhinoceros in the city's north. The *Chronicles of Huayang* records: Li Bing made stone rhinoceros outside the city to control water monsters. The area south of the stone rhinoceros' town is named Rhinoceros Li ... West twenty-seven of Xipu County is the past twenty-four townships, now twenty. In the second year of the Chuigong Reign, the court divided the western suburbs of Chengdu and set up Xipu County, probably because of the stone rhinoceros made by Li Bing. The name of the county comes from this.

After that, there were 36 written historical records until the Qing Dynasty. The content of the texts is similar, with details such as the size of the stone rhinoceros, its orientation, its location in Chengdu, temples, changes in the city gates, and urban changes. Interestingly, the Japanese Yamakawa Hayamizu recorded in *Bashu · City Historical Sites · Stone Cow*: "There is a stone cow in the higher school, which is extremely strange and ancient in production. It is about four feet long and three feet high. Although it is damaged everywhere, all four legs are intact, and the face and nose still exist. Nearby the hall is a temple called Shi Niu Temple, built in the Han Dynasty, and it is the Shengshou Temple in ancient times. According to *Sichuan General Records*, a stone rhinoceros is made by Li Bing, the Governor of Shu, in the temple. The *Commentary on the Water Classic* says: 'Li Bing made five stone rhinoceros, two in the house, one in the market bridge, two sunk in the abyss.' The one placed in the school today is suspected of being one of the two heads of the house. In addition, the one in front of the Daci Temple may be the other. If this is true, it is all from the Han Dynasty. This can be compelling material for studying the stone carvings of that year."

Since then, there have been many accounts. "If ordinary stones are considered having general sorcerous potency because of their common properties such as weight and hardness, then special stones are considered having special sorcerous potency because of their special shape or color."[1] It is also of particular significance that the stones used for water ruling were carved in the shape of rhinoceroses and cows, probably mainly to simulate and inherit the ancient ritual of "seeking the year in the river" and sinking the cows. Influence, the stone rhinoceros (bull) is equivalent to Li Bing. By the principle of homeopathic sorcery, Li Bing's governance of floods to subdue the demon is naturally considered passing to the body of the stone rhinoceros (bull), the stone statue of Li Bing in the Eastern Han Dynasty on the precise point of the inscription is the best circumstantial evidence.

---

1. James George Frazer, *The Golden Bough: A Study in Comparative Religion*, 4th edition, Chapter 3, "Sympathetic Sorcery."

———— ◆ ————

CHAPTER 12

The Stone Statue of the Weir Worker
May Be Dayu

Next to the "Beijiangpeng" (the official name of Dujiangyan in the Eastern Han Dynasty), a large "Three Fairy Stone Men," or three stone statues of gods, was carved and erected by the officials of the Eastern Han Dynasty for flood control of the Min River. One stone figure was unearthed in 1974. It can be identified as Li Bing (both Governor of Shu and God of Shen) by placing the inscriptions on it.

In 1975, another stone figure was unearthed about 37 meters away from where the statue of Li Bing was found, with no head and holding a shovel with both hands, which some experts later called the stone statue of Weir Worker (now exhibited together with the stone statue of Li Bing in the Fulongguan of the Dujiangyan scenic spot). We have reason to suspect that it is also a stone statue of the "Three Fairy Stone Men." Probably it is Yu the Great.

Records of the Grand Historian · Treatise on Rivers and Waterways earlier compares Yu the Great with Li Bing, inadvertently setting a precedent for future generations to praise Li Bing for his "meritorious work after the divine Yu." Li Bing and Yu the Great are also very similar. Yu the Great is excellent at geography and the river's pulse. Li Bing can observe and understand the regulations of water flow. Both are famous for water management; both are superheroes who have transformed water hazards into water conservancy; both have "locked water monsters," both have been associated with Shu, and both have undergone a process of upgrading from human to god.

Han Feizi, a document of the Warring States period, said, "Yu, the king of the world, was the one who held farming tools and put the people first." This classic image of Yu has been expressed in many pictures in later times, none more famous than a Han portrait stone at the Wuliang Temple in Shandong. The stone is richly illustrated, like a page from a comic strip. The portrait shows Xia Yu wearing a short robe and a pointed straw hat, with his left hand raised and his right hand holding a straight-handled "two-edged shovel" (the name is found in the Eastern Han document *Explaining Simple and Analyzing Compound Characters*). This portrait is reminiscent of the modern sculpture of Yu the Great in Wenchuan, still with the right hand holding the separator. This is also the same Yu the Great in the minds of the Chinese people, passed down from generation to generation and unchanged throughout the ages.

Unlike the portrait at the Wuliang Temple, the shovel held by the stone figure unearthed in 1975 is not a two-edged shovel but a concave shovel, carved in stone but with lines of metal edges, similar in shape and longer in length to the iron-tipped wooden shovel found in the fill of the Mawangdui No. 3 Han tomb in Changsha, Hunan. The discovery of this stone figure within Dujiangyan proves again that the shovel was an essential tool in the construction of agricultural water conservancy; as Yan Shigu said, "The shovel is used for digging the drains." Looking at it, we can fully imagine the grand scene of the ancestors. "Millions of them raised the shovel like clouds, and in the ditch release, people jumped for joy, playing with the clear stream, raising the water like a happy rain to moisten the dry earth and moisten people's hearts." (*Book of Han*, Volume 29, "Treatise on Rivers and Canals")

A stone figurine of the Eastern Han Dynasty holding the shovel was excavated in Emei, Sichuan, smaller than the one in Dujiangyan, but with a head in a hat and a concave shovel. In addition to these artistic images, many physical objects are unearthed. In the special exhibition *The Land of Abundance and the Silk Road* at the Chengdu Museum, there are several pieces of the iron shovel from the Eastern Han Dynasty unearthed along the "Southern Silk Road," all with the words "Shu Prefecture" and "Chengdu" on them. During the Han Dynasty, the concave shovel was a typical and popular production tool in Sichuan. Therefore, the grafting of the open shovel onto Xia Yu's body by Han Dynasty stone sculptors was just a reference to and a reflection of reality.

CHAPTER 13

Li Bing in the Documents of the Two Han Dynasties

Western Han Dynasty

Before the Western Han Dynasty, Li Bing was unknown.

Records of the Grand Historian · Treatise on Rivers and Waterways is the earliest documentary record of Li Bing. Sima Qian (135–90 BCE) contains only eighteen key characters in the book: "蜀守冰凿离碓辟沫水之害穿二江成都之中." It means Li Bing, the Governor of Shu, excavated the Lidui to exclude the great flood and excavated the Pi and Jian Rivers directly to Chengdu.

Referring to *Chronicles of Huayang,* we can see that the chiseling of the Lidui is only taking part in the whole. This one link refers to the entire project building Dujiangyan. Frankly, Li Bing's performance in Chengdu is much more than this (details below).

Volume Seven of *Baikong Liutie* cited this sentence from *Records of the Grand Historian* as "蜀守李冰凿离堆山辟暴水之害穿二江灌成都中." Volume 37 of *Yuding Yuanjian Lei Han* cited it as "蜀守李冰凿离堆山辟暴水之害穿二江灌成都城." These two texts can be regarded as a supplement and explanation of *Records of the Grand Historian · Treatise on Rivers and Waterways.*

First, they mentioned the full name of Li Bing. Second, they explained the meaning of 沫水 *Moshui*, which was 暴水 *Pushui*. In the *Classic of Poetry*, 暴 is a text of "终风且暴." In *Explaining Simple and Analyzing Compound Character*, it is 瀑 *Pu*, which means rainstorm. 沫 *Mo* is another saying. The flood after the rapid rain, that is, the 暴水 *Pushui* or 沫水 *Moshui*. Third, Li Bing's main achievement, besides creating Dujiangyan, was to change the pattern of the city of Chengdu. Li Bing excavated the Pi and Jian Rivers directly to Chengdu City and built seven bridges on the two rivers.

In summary, the eighteen characters in *Records of the Grand Historian · Treatise on Rivers and Waterways* should be punctuated with two parallel clauses: "蜀守冰凿离碓, 辟沫水之害; 穿二江, (灌)成都之中." We should add 灌 *Guan* before 成都 *Chengdu*.

After Sima Qian, Li Bing is mentioned in the book of Yang Xiong (53–18 BCE), a native of Chengdu. The complete *Biographies of the Kings of Shu* were lost, and only some fragments remain because other ancient books have been cited to preserve the present. There are two such records involving Li Bing. First, "The rivers of Shu flooded, and the people suffered. Governor Li Bing made five stone rhinoceros: put two in the city, one under the bridge, and two in the water, to tame the water demon;"[1] Second, "Li Bing was appointed Governor of Shu Prefecture in the State of Qin. He said Wen Mountain was the Tianpeng Pass, called the Tianpeng Gate. The dead passed through here. Ghosts and spirits repeatedly appeared."[2] These two articles were later absorbed by Chang Qu, who was also a native of Chengdu, into the *Chronicles of Huayang*, which is a logical sequence in time and space.

Reading through the section "King Xiaowen of Qin took Li Bing as the Governor of Shu" to the section "One in the River" in the *Chronicles of Huayang*, we can connect the above-quoted *Records of the Grand Historian · Treatise on Rivers and Waterways* and the *Biographies of the Kings of Shu* to arrive at the following events.

Li Bing was the Governor of Shu during the Qin Dynasty and called Wen Mountain Tianpeng Pass, or Tianpeng Gate, where all the dead

---

1. *The Literature Collection of Ancient and Modern Affairs*, Volume 36. The original text is "Li Yang Bing." The word *Yang* is derivative, so delete it.
2. *Taiping Huanyu Ji*, vol. 73.

passed, and the ghosts and spirits appeared repeatedly. Then he sacrificed the river, dug the river, and made the levees. He cut the Lidui to prevent the harm of the stormy water, penetrated the two rivers, and filled Chengdu; he made five stone rhinoceroses: two in the city, one under the bridge, and two in the water to tame the water spirits.

Eastern Han Dynasty

By the Eastern Han Dynasty, more literature on Li Bing was written.

Ban Gu (32–92 CE, a first-century poet and historian) basically copied the "Treatise on Rivers and Waterways" to his *Book of Han*, but with slight additions and changes: adding "蜀守冰" as "蜀守李冰"; changing 左 "石" 右 "隹" 之堆 to 上 "山" 下 "隹" 之堆, both of which are the ancient character of "堆"; changing "成都之中" to "成都中."

In Cui Shi's *Argument of Politics*, it is said that "Li Bing of Shu Prefecture cut the Lidui and opened the two rivers, which is still relied on by Yizhou."[3] Although implicitly affirming Li Bing's merits, the caliber is consistent with the "Treatise on Rivers and Waterways," except that the official title is omitted.

In the first year of the Jianning Regin (168), the *Inscription on the Idol of Li Bing, the Governor of Shu in Qin Dynasty* (The author's proposed title. Interpretation of the text can see *Cultural Relics*, vol. 7 in 1974.) shows that the statue of Li Bing has been included in the "Three Fairy of the Stone Men." It can be seen at the latest in the Jianning Regin Li Bing has been deified.

In the third year of the Xiping Regin (174), the *Ode to Zhou Fujun, Governor of Guiyang, Han Dynasty* (dated according to *Jin Shi Lu*, vol. 1, and the name of the tablet according to vol. 16) restores the ancient name of "蜀守冰," which proves that the "Treatise on Rivers and Waterways" is not an isolated case. The term "犂雉" means Lidui, and "殄終止犂雉" means "chiseling Lidui."

Cai Yong's *Eulogy of Fanhui Canal of Jingzhao* does not directly identify the water conservancy projects built by Li Bing and others. Still, it points out their basic principles at a high level: "A wise gentleman will develop agricultural production and build various water conservation projects by the laws of nature,

---

3. *Sibu Congkan*, Chinese Academy of Arts and Sciences, borrowed from the Song Dynasty edition of *Imperial Reader of the Taiping Era*, the *Imperial Library of Japan Collection* by Tofukuji, Kyoto. Now it is at Seikadō Bunko Art Museum, Tokyo.

depending on the fertility of the land. In this way, the country can be rich, and the people can be happy, which has been the truth since ancient times. Just as Ximen Bao built a water conservancy in Ye, Zheng Guo built Zhengguo Canal in Qin, and Li Bing built Dujiangyan in Sichuan, capable ministers governed the country by following this principle."[4]

The story of Li Bing, recorded in Ying Shao's *Comprehensive Meaning of Customs and Mores*, is strongly mythological and not only coincides with but also corroborates the *Inscription of the Idol of Li Bing, the Governor of Shu in the Qin Dynasty*. The original text has been lost and was earlier quoted in the *Commentary on the Water Classic* as follows.

> King Zhao of Qin sent Li Bing as the Governor of Shu and opened the river as a weir to irrigate ten-thousand hectares of farmland. The god of the river was terrible and wanted to take two women on earth as his wives. Li Bing sent his daughters to the river god's shrine and then persuaded the river god to drink wine. The god's cup was shaken only slightly, and the wine did not decrease. Then Li Bing sternly scolded, and the river god disappeared at once. After a long time, only to see two cows fighting on the riverbank. Got an opening, Li Bing came back sweating. He said to his subordinates: "I'm too tired to fight; shouldn't you help me out? The bull with the white ribbon around his waist to the south is me!" A moment later, the two cows fought again, and Li Bing's subordinate stabbed the bull in the north, the god of the river. He died on the spot. The Shu people admired Li Bing's heroic spirit, and all the strong and healthy people were named "Bing'er."[5]

This river water divinity and the previous quote Yang Xiong so-called "water essence" can be echoed. The Li Bing's first years as the Governor of Shu were designated as "King Zhao of Qin" in the *Comprehensive Meaning of Customs and Mores*, which is slightly different from the "King Xiaowen of Qin" in the *Chronicles of Huayang* and has more influence. However, considering the difference between history and mythology, it seems that the *Chronicles of Huayang* is the right one.

---

4. *The Chronicle of Eastern Han Dynasty*, vol. 23.

5. *Commentary on the Water Classic*, vol. 33, *Sibu Congkan, a Collection of Shanghai Hanfen Hall, the Selected Edition of Wuying Palace Hall*.

The Eastern Han people regarded Li Bing as a "wisdom and intelligence gentleman" or even a "god," and his idolatry and mythological rendering began from then on. Even more remarkable is that they clearly understood the engineering principles and historical orientation of Li Bing's Dujiangyan.

—◆◆—

CHAPTER 14

Li Bing's Journey to the Altar of God

In 250 BCE, Li Bing, the Governor of Shu Prefecture, who had served the Chengdu Plain for many generations, entered the stage of history. About his deeds, *Records of the Grand Historia* only has one sentence: "Li Bing, the Governor of Shu, excavated the Lidui to exclude the great flood and excavated the Pi and Jian Rivers directly to Chengdu." It was not until the *Chronicles of Huayang* came out that the image of Li Bing was gradually fleshed out.

Li Bing Was a Man in the Warring States Period

It is said that when he first came to Shu, Li Bing was not busy with water management but first observed the mountains. Li Bing, who "knew astronomy and geography" and also knew *feng shui*, saw the Mount Mins on both sides of the river facing each other like a gate, so he called the mountain "Tianpeng Que" (also known as "Tianpeng Gate," "Pengmen Que"), and said, "Dead people pass through here, and ghosts and spirits appear everywhere." Because he "seemed to see the gods," he saw these dead people with his own eyes.

These dead people are the dead Shu people; they are lying in coffins and buried deep underground, wading upstream is only their spirits, specifically as "ghosts and spirits." After death, the Shu people are buried in a coffin. They believe the coffin is the boat carrying the soul, which can help their souls cross the rolling river and then return to their hometown and reunion with the soul of their ancestors. This hometown is not elsewhere, and it is the birthplace of ancient Shu, the first king of Shu, Cancong's hometown—the upper reaches of the Min River in the western plateau of Sichuan.

To gain the trust and support of the Shu people along the Min River, Li Bing "then set up three sacrifices from the water, with three animals, *gui*, and *bi*. Then sink these into the river." The three places of sacrifice were set up on the Min River, and then the shamans were ordered to sink the cattle, sheep, pigs, *gui*, and *bi* into the water, ostensibly to sacrifice the dead of Shu related to water management, such as Bieling, but actually to offer the river or river gods. *Chronicles of Huayang* cited *Records of the Grand Historian · Treatise on Sacrifices*, "Li Bing, the Governor of Shu set up three shrines of river gods in Pengmen Que."

In ancient rituals, 埋 *Mai* is the concept of sacrificial mountains and forests. It means "buried." 沈 *Chen* is for the sacrificial river, which means "sink." Sanxingdui sacrificial pit is a buried sacrifice, and Li Bing took sunk sacrifice. The object of sacrifice is different, and the sacrificial rites will be different.

After the river sacrifice, Li Bing cut to the chase: "congestion river for the weirs." This was the main and most important task he had to perform as the Governor of Shu. In the ancient Shu dialect, a weir was called a Peng, and the Peng made by Li Bing was the earliest Dujiangyan, borrowing from the ancient method of the Shu people to congest the river with "bamboo cages and stones."

In addition to making the weirs, Li Bing carved three stone figures and stood them in three streams of water, creating a pact with the river gods: "When the water level is low, the feet of the stone figures should not be lowered, and when it is high, the shoulders of the stone figures should not be higher." In fact, this agreement is the inscription engraved on the body of the stone man; the stone man is only a human-shaped "Water Level Gauge," unknowingly playing a role in monitoring the water level of the Min River.

Besides making stone man, Li Bing "made five stone rhinoceros," the purpose is "to tame the water spirit." Because once it makes waves, the Min River will flood into a disaster.

Li Bing Is God in the Han and Jin Dynasties

Li Bing's water management deeds were more divine since the Eastern Han Dynasty.

Li Bing was gradually pushed up to the high altar of god. For example, the matter of making stone rhinoceros transformed into a bullfighting myth.

"King Zhao of Qin sent Li Bing as the Governor of Shu and opened the river as a weir to irrigate ten-thousand hectares of farmland. The god of the river was bad and wanted to take two women on earth as his wives. Li Bing sent his daughters to the river god's shrine and then persuaded the river god to drink wine. The god's cup was shaken only slightly, and the wine did not decrease. Then, Li Bing sternly scolded, and the river god disappeared at once. After a long time, only to see two cows fighting on the riverbank. Got an opening, Li Bing came back sweating, and he said to his subordinates: "I'm too tired to fight; shouldn't you help me out? The bull with the white ribbon around his waist to the south is me!" A moment later, the two cows fought again, and Li Bing's subordinate stabbed the bull in the north, the god of the river."

This story is from a book of the Eastern Han Dynasty, called *Comprehensive Meaning of Customs and Mores*, by Ying Shao, who was also a prefecture governor (Taishan Prefecture Governor of the Eastern Han Dynasty).

After the death of the god of the river, the plain of Chengdu was "free from drought and floods, and great harvest every year." It was not long before the reputation of "Heavenly Mansion" spread. Li Bing turned into a bull, dueled with the bull-shaped river god, and finally won, but it was just an alternative expression of building a weir to control the floods.

Besides written records, there was also an official campaign to create gods in the Eastern Han Dynasty. In 168 CE (the first year of the Jianning, Emperor Ling's Reign), Yin Longchang and Chen Yi, following the old example of Li Bing, who made three stone figures to make a contract with the river god, carved the "Three Fairy of Stone Men" to "tame the water for many generations." A Li Bing is nearly three meters high among the stone men. The middle of its lapel inscription says, "His Excellency Li Bing, The Former Governor of Shu Prefecture," which is obviously a combination of humans and god.

Until the Eastern Jin Dynasty, the Leshan area also had the legend of Li Bing fighting water gods: "At that time, a great flood broke out in the Qingyi River. The flood came down through Mount Meng and flooded the land. When it reached Nan'an, the rivers merged. The water level kept rising, and all could touch the cliffs on both sides of the river, and the current was so fast that all the boats on the water were washed away. Such floods have occurred since successive dynasties. Li Bing dispatched soldiers and craftsmen to flatten the cliffs on both sides of the river and widen and correct the waterway. There is also a story: "When Li Bing cut the cliffs, the water god got angry. So, Li Bing took his sword, jumped into the water, fought with the water god, and defeated him. To this day, the people of Leshan are still enjoying the happiness of Li Bing's victory."

Regarding "The water god got angry," *Xu Bo Wu Zhi* has a slightly different saying: "The river god Bi gets angry." Specifying the water god as Bi should already be a rendition of the Song Dynasty.

Li Bing's Sage in Tang Dynasty

In the Tang Dynasty, the images of Li Bing and the river god became dragons one after another, and the previous bullfight also randomly became a bull-dragon fight and a dragon fight.

Once upon a time, the river god turned into a dragon to make mischief and drowned many people. Li Bing took the form of a bull, fought with it, and could not overcome it. So, he jumped out of the water and chose hundreds of warriors, each with a powerful bow and big arrows, to scare the dragon back. The thunder and wind rose briefly, and the sky and earth turned black. Two bulls were fighting on the river when the wind and thunder were slight. Seeing the opportunity, the warriors shot the river god with no white belt around his waist. From then on, the Shu people were no longer trapped by the water. "So far, the big waves rushed in and seemed to flood the Li Bing Temple, full of retreat. That's why the local custom of bullfighting is held every spring and winter. This custom should come from it." Thousands of families in the south of Li Bing Temple are near the river, and even if the water rises in autumn, they are still safe because "there is a stone bull under the temple." In the fifth year of the Dahe Reign of the Tang Dynasty (831), the great flood broke out again. The god of Li Bing transformed into a dragon and again fought against the dragon-like river god. In the end, Zoumian and Zitong were all flooded, and the water damage affected dozens of counties, but the area of Chengdu was safe.

This story is from *Records of Chengdu* by Lu Qiu of the Tang Dynasty. There are shades of *Comprehensive Meanings of Customs and Mores* and interpretations and developments from the Tang Dynasty. It is interesting to note that when scholars today trace the origin of Sichuan Opera, they often cite the phrase, "That's why the local custom of bullfighting is held every spring and winter." According to Lu Qiu's speculation, the bullfighting drama before the Tang Dynasty was imitated from the story of Li Bing's bullfight. Is this the case? I'm afraid it's only a suspicious case of "something happened for a reason, but no solid evidence." However, "there is a stone bull under the temple" may be one of the five stone rhinoceroses, which again supports the myth of bullfighting and the historical fact that Li Bing made stone rhinoceroses have a specific causal relationship.

In the fifteenth year of the Guangzheng Era (952), Meng Chang, the Later Lord of Later Shu, ordered the drama troupe to rehearse the play of gods arrayed at Guankou and two dragons fighting. It seems to be regarded as the stream of the bullfighting play.

Li Bing Fights the River God and the Persian God of Rain against the Drought Demon

In *Comprehensive Meanings of Customs and Mores*, Li Bing fights with the bull. In the *Records of Chengdu*, Li Bing kills a dragon. These are not what a mortal man can do; even if a person is strong and healthy, he cannot fight a god. So, Li Bing, who opposed the bull and killed the dragon, was not the Governor of Shu in the *Records of the Grand Historian*. He was given divinity and transformed into a god.

Li Bing was very similar to Yu the Great, who was "good at geography and waters," and Li Bing could "know the water veins." Both are famous for their water management, have "locked the water monster," are related to Sichuan, and both were upgraded from human to god.

Personnel have similarities, from the transformation of myths and legends from personnel, if similar, of course, is inevitable. The saying goes, "People share the same heart and the same reasoning; in the past and the present, there is no exception." Huang Zhigang and Qian Zhongshu pointed out early on that many stories of snake fighting and dragon fighting in the Tang and Song dynasties had many similarities with the legend of Li Bing's bullfighting recorded in the *Comprehensive Meaning of Customs and Mores*.

Some contemporary scholars believe that the story of Li Bing slaying a dragon is similar in plot to the story of *Avesta*, the holy book of Zoroastrianism. Tishtrya, the Persian god of rain, fought against the drought-bring demon in the book.

The majestic Tishtrya, in the form of a white stallion with golden ears and a gold bridle, landed on the river Farah Kart. But Apaosha, the drought-bring demon, swung into a black bald horse with bald ears, a bald neck, and bald tail, a hideous black bald horse and came to meet him. Tishtrya fought with Apaosha, and they fought for three days and nights. Apaosha was able to defeat Tishtrya.

After his defeat, Tishtrya cried out to Ahura Mazda, the Creator, that if he could not defeat the drought-bring demon, the rivers would be cut off, the grass would wither, and the earth would suffer shame and disaster. He appealed to people to offer sacrifices to him to help him replenish his strength: "If people mention my name in their prayers and praise me as they call upon and praise other gods, then I will gain the power of ten horses, ten camels, ten cows, ten mountains and ten great navigable rivers."

Ahura Mazda heard his appeal and called upon the people to offer sacrifices to Tishtrya, so Tishtrya regained his strength, reverted to a white steed with golden ears, dressed for battle, and fought the drought-bring demon Apaosha for three days and nights, finally driving away the drought-bring demon and restoring the earth to live: "O earth! Beaming with joy! The waters of the earth's rivers flowed freely, sending large seeds to the fields and small seeds to the pastures and on to the four corners of the world."

The Persian god of rain lost the first battle against the drought-bring demon and was replenished by the sacrifices people offered to him, and only after the second battle did he defeat the drought-bring demon; the fight of Li Bing in *Records of Chengdu* was also lost in the first battle, and Li Bing surfaced and asked people to help him, and dove again to slay the dragon before he finally won. Tishtrya's opponent is a drought-bring demon, and Li Bing's opponent is a water monster, which is precisely the opposite. Still, Tishtrya expels the drought-bring demon, and Li Bing cuts the dragon to make the rivers flow peacefully and water the earth. The drought in Persia and the lack of rain make people regard the drought-bring demon as the devil, and the rivers in Sichuan are so rampant that people feel the water monster is a plague. Although the characters are set differently, the story's structure is consistent.[1]

In fact, in Sichuan during the Qing Dynasty, Li Bing was already regarded as a proper Chinese god of rain. In Danyi County, Li Bing is worshipped on the 24th day of the 6th month of the lunar calendar. If there is a drought, everyone will greet the Li Bing's tablet together to pray for rain. The people will perform a

---

1. Xiao Bing, *The Original and Transmutation of the Story of Erlang Shen.* Liu Zongdi, *Erlang Rides a White Horse from Persia.*

play to thank the gods if the wish is fulfilled. Fuling also pays homage to Li Bing, the Lord of Sichuan, on the 24th day of the 6th lunar month. The prayer for rain is answered immediately whenever there is a drought.

The Image of Li Bing in the Song Dynasty

Li Bing's story has more tragic colors, from the Xianping to Jiayou of the Northern Song Dynasty (998–1063): "Li Bing fought with water monsters, but he died after failing to win the fight. Since then, the Min River has no more floods. Dragons and sea monsters were hidden, and people lived peaceful lives." Water monsters are dragons and others, but Li Bing was defeated and died. This is the record by Song Qi, the governor of Chengdu. Since Li Bing died, there would naturally be a tomb shrine, and the *New Book of Tang*, which Song Qi took part in compiling, says that "there is a Li Bing shrine mountain" in Shifang. (According to Cao Xuequan of the Ming Dynasty, "There is the Ascension Terrace on it, where Li Bing ascended.")

Another local deity, Li Erlang, emerged during the Yuanfeng period (1078–1085 CE). During the reign of Emperor Shenzong of the Song Dynasty, a shrine to Erlang Shen was built in the west of the capital city of Dongjing (now Kaifeng, Henan Province), one *li* outside the Gate of Wansheng. This Erlang Shen is said to be the son of Li Bing, the Prince of Guangji in Yongkang Daojiang County (now Dujiangyan City).

Later, the emperor gave the shrine the name "Shenbao Guan," so Li Erlang was also known as the "God of Shenbao Guan." On the 24th day of the sixth month of each lunar year, which is said to be his birthday, Shenbao Guan has the largest number of incense and various juggling performances from dawn to dusk.

The scale of the festival naturally increased in Guankou, the place of his fame (present-day Dujiangyan City). As Zhu Xi (1130–1200) said: "The Temple of Erlang in Guankou County, Sichuan Province, was established because Li Bing excavated the Lidui, which the people merited. Later, there were many spirits and monsters, and it was his second son. In the beginning, Erlang was sealed as a king by the court. Emperor Huizong worshipped Taoism, saying he was a true monarch, so he changed the title to Erlang as a true monarch … Every year, each family competes to pay tribute to see who has more sheep to offer. In this way, it killed tens of thousands of sheep each time, resulting in a mountain of bones in front of the temple of Erlang. The government also received tax money."

Fan Chengda (1126–1193), who worked as an official in Chengdu, wrote a poem called *Lidui Xing*, which confirms Zhu Xi's words:

> The peaks are so steep, like two reclining tigers.
> With an ax, Li Bing chops away at the Lidui
> and leaves traces like fish scales behind.
> No one dares to disturb the emerald waters of the pool.
> There is a fierce dragon locking it away with iron locks.
> The river is diverted and injected into the stone gate,
> and Japonica rice in Sichuan grows as plentiful as yellow clouds.
> Fifty thousand sheep were sacrificed for the grand ceremony.
> And spring and autumn drums fill the air with pale smoke roots.
> I have taken up my post as an agricultural official.
> I came every year to inspect the Xijiang River.
> Fried rice in Chengdu is not expensive.
> Officials would join me in the bustling silkworm market.
> We knocked on every door to taste their wine.
> Pepper and cinnamon wine removed the stickiness,
> I would like to say a word that god would not hear:
> "Can we love sheep as much as we love people?"
>
> —FAN CHENGDA, *Lidui Xing*

Before the poem, there is a preface: "Along the river, there are two interrupted cliffs, and it is said that Li Bing, the Governor of Shu, cut this mountain away to separate the river. It is also said that Li locked the sinful dragon in the pond, and now there is Fulongguan in the pond. When there was a drought in Sichuan, the water of the rivers dried up, and the government immediately sent officials here to offer sacrifices, so the water in Dujiangyan could be self-sufficient. The people took part in a sacrificial competition to see who had more sheep to offer, and 40,000 to 50,000 sheep were killed yearly."

The place where the two cliffs are interrupted is the Baopingkou between the present Yulei Mountain and the Lidui. There is a pool next to the Baopingkou and a temple on the pool, both named "Fulong." According to legend, Li Bing had locked the sinful dragon under the Lidui and put it in the cold pool, so it was called "Fulong," which means "subduing the evil dragon."

Wang Xiangzhi's *Yudi Jisheng* quoted the Northern Song Dynasty scholar Li Zhu's *Biography of Li Bing's Water Management.*

"Li Bing, the Governor of Shu, and his son combined their efforts to capture the strong demon dragon. The dragon was locked up in the Lidui and called the Fulong Pond. Later, he built the Fulongguan on top of the pond."

The details of killing sheep and sacrifice, Fan Chengda explained in his book, *Wu Chuan Lu.*

"Governor Li dredged the river, drove the dragon, and made a great contribution to Sichuan. The people were grateful for his merits, and many people visited his temple to worship. It is said that 50,000 sheep are killed every year for worship. Every commoner would buy a sheep to pay tribute to Li Bing. Those whose families occasionally produced lambs did not dare to keep them but still drove them to the temple and killed them for worship. In front of the Li Bing Temple are dozens of hundreds of butchers. The financial income of Yongkang Prefecture mainly depends on the tax revenue from killing sheep. Such a sacrifice is too much!"

The word "drive the dragon" can be far from echoing the storyline in *Comprehensive Meaning of Customs and Mores* and *Records of Chengdu*, and the lock dragon should be a derivative version of the Song Dynasty. The temple was then called "Chongde Temple," that is, the predecessor of Two Kings Temple. On June 24 of every lunar year, people had to buy a sheep each and bring it to the temple for sacrifice. Even small lambs were not spared. In front of the temple, there are dozens of hundreds of butchers. They killed the sheep to accumulate bones as a mountain. The local government levied a tax on this, and it became the primary financial revenue.

To be especially clear, regarding the object of killing sheep sacrifice, Fan Chengda said it was Li Bing, and Zhu Xi said it was Erlang Shen. Now the Taoists of Two Kings Temple will grandly celebrate the "birth anniversary of the Ture Monarch of Qingyuan Miaodao" on the 24th day of the 6th lunar month. The Ture Monarch also refers to the Erlang Shen. But folk don't know what the "birth anniversary of the Ture Monarch of Qingyuan Miaodao is," generally said to be Li Bing's birthday. Li Bing and Erlang Shen have been confused since the Southern Song Dynasty.

Sinful Dragon Looking at His Mother

In the Qing Dynasty, Li Bing was no longer the only one who had defeated the dragon.

Yang Chaoguan's *Erlang Shen First Appearing in Guankou* (also known as *Li Lang Subdues Zhupo Dragon*) is a miscellaneous drama about Li Bing's excavation of the Lidui, which broke the dragon cave, and the mother and son of the dragon "changed their bodies" and came out to seek revenge and kill Li Bing. The mother and son of the dragon "hanged the green silk on the horns," while Li Bing "hung the raw red silk on the helmet." Li Bing was outnumbered, so he asked his son Erlang to rescue him. Erlang intercepted out, bent his bow, released arrows, and released his divine eagle and whistling dog.

Finally, he captured the two dragons who got help from the wind, thunder, rain, and lightning, the gods of the six Ding and six Jia.[2] Li locked the mother of the dragon under the Lidui and commanded her to restrain the river's waves. The water shall not exceed the shoulder when it is deep and shall not be lower than the foot when it is shallow. After that, Li put the son of the dragon in the Baopingkou and told him to guard the water gate. The dragon swallowed the water and spitted to fill the farmland so that a thousand miles of barren land would be turned into fertile land and become the land of abundance forever.

Within the quotation from Yuan Mei's *Suiyuan Suibi*, the way Li Bing asked his son to do so was by entrusting him with a dream: "Bing, as the prefecture governor, took the form of a bull and entered the water to kill the dragon, and the fight was not won. So, he sent a dream to his son, who entered the water to help his father kill the dragon."

In Li Diaoyuan's *Jing Wa Za Ji*, Li Bing locking sinful dragon evolved into the Erlang locking sinful dragon: "Fulongguan is on the top of Lidui. A deep pool is under the Fulongguan. Some people say that Erlang locks sinful dragons in it. The lock may sometimes be seen when the frost and water are fallen."

---

2. 六丁六甲神 The gods of the six Ding and six Jia were originally the gods of the heavenly stems and earthly branches, and their gods were twelve, equivalent to the six aces and six bases of the sixty Taisui generals in the later period. The oracle bone inscriptions of the Shang Dynasty already had records of the sixty aces. In the Han Dynasty, there was already the worship of the six Ding and six Jia in the *Notes on the Qi Ju of Emperor Xian*. The six gods of Ding are Ding Mao, Ding Si, Ding Wei, Ding You, Ding Hai, and Ding Chou. The six gods of Jia are Jia Zi, Jia Xu, Jia Shen, Jia Wu, Jia Chen, and Jia Yin.

A little later, the legend of Wangniang Beach circulated. Li Bing and Erlang, father and son, are all together on the battlefield, but the sinful dragon becomes the main character. At the end of the Qing Dynasty, the novel *A Tale of The Eight Immortals* was slightly mentioned in the section "Two Dragon Tears Spilled into the Wangniang Beach," while the complete story appeared in the Republican period, which is roughly as follows.

In the past, a filial son in Guan County was poor and mowed grass to serve his mother. God sympathized with his filial piety and gave him a bush of grass cut and reborn every day. The boy felt terrific and started digging from the ground of the sacred grass. He found a large pearl on the ground and hid it in a rice casket. The next day, he opened the casket and saw the rice was full. He put it in the money box, and it was full of money. The family became rich. The neighbors were surprised and knew the reason, then asked to see the pearl. But after they gathered around, they came together to grab the pearl. The boy was terrified, so he put it into his mouth. The pearl rolled into his belly; he was thirsty for a drink. Drinking up a tank of water, he still did not feel enough, so he drank in the river. When his mother chased him, she saw he had turned into a dragon, but only one foot had not yet changed. The mother persisted in chasing after her son, saying in grief, "You are a sinful dragon!" So, he made waves and went away with the river. However, he still looked back frequently at his mother. The place where he looked back became a big beach, leaving "twelve beaches of wangniang" or "twenty-four beaches of wangniang" of the remains. Wangniang means looking at his mother.

The dragon, hating the persecution of the villagers, unleashed a flood to take revenge.

Later, Li Bing fought with the dragon to subdue it, and his son Erlang supported him. The dragon could not win and disappeared into human form. There was a Lady Wang, the phantom form of Guanyin Bodhisattva, who helped Bing capture the dragon and set up a noodle store by the roadside. The dragon was hungry to eat noodles, but the noodles transformed into iron locks. The dragon was locked and tied to iron stakes in a deep pool, so the name of the temple was called "Fulongguan."[3]

---

3. Lin Mingjun, *Sichuan Water Governor and Water Gods*, Huang Zhigang, *The Water Gods of China*, Chapters 2 and 14.

Why do we need to use iron stakes to lock the dragon? It is said that dragons are naturally afraid of iron. In the fifteen years of the Guangzheng Era (952 CE), Guankou County reported the Min River rose, and the iron pillar for locking the dragons frequently felt vibration." Chen Bingkui's *The Song of Dujiangyan* said, "People in the Ming Dynasty purchased iron to build the pillars, and the reign title of the Wanli Emperor was engraved on the pillars." The text was *The Pillar of Yongzhen Puji in the fourth year of the Wanli Reign. Yongzhen Puji* means to lock the dragon forever and save the people of the world. Another saying is, "Zhao Dai and Wang Teng, two officials, ordered to pour stones into the water, set up the stakes, wrap iron chains, and tighten the ancient pillars firmly tethered lock." The story of the iron stakes and iron locks of the dragon may be due to this.

The story of Erlang assisting Li Bing in his fight with the dragon is apparently derived from the story of his subordinates helping Li Bing in the *Comprehensive Meaning of Customs and Mores* and *Records of Chengdu*. It seems to be inferred from this that Li Erlang was, in fact, a subordinate of Li Bing. In *Comprehensive Meanings of Customs and Mores*, they can be called *Guanshu* or *Zhubu*. In *Records of Chengdu*, they are called brave soldiers or warriors.

CHAPTER 15

Erlang Shen of Guankou

I

There are at least three sets of candidates for the title of "Guankou Erlang" in history: Li Erlang, Zhao Erlang, and Yang Erlang. The reason I say three sets, rather than three, is that some names often cover more than one person, such as Li Bing and Li Bing's son, who were both nicknamed "Erlang" (the two were combined in the Northern Song Dynasty), and Yang Mo and Yang Jian, who were both probably "Yang Erlang." In addition, the exploits of Li Erlang, Zhao Erlang, and Yang Erlang are often confused and entangled, ultimately making their relationship inextricable.

Zan Ning (919–1001 CE) mentioned "the temple of Li Bing, the god of Yulei Mountain in Daojiang" in Volume 6 of the *Biographies of the Eminent Monks of Song Dynasty*, pointing out that the temple site is on top of Yulei Mountain. Volume 8 of *Longping Ji* by Zeng Gong recorded, "The Shu people hold a temple fair every year to worship Li Bing in Guankou."

Volume 73 of the *Universal Geography of the Taiping Era* by Yue Shi (930–1007) recorded, "To the west of the town of Guankou is the Shrine of the Lady Jade, and to the west of the Shrine of the Lady Jade is the Li Bing Temple." It is unknown whether the Shrine of the Lady Jade and the "Lady Jade Room" of the *Chronicles of Huayang* refer to the same place.

Records of Ancient and Modern Chengdu by Zhao Bian (1008–1084) stated: "Li Bing sent his son, Erlang, to build three stone men to manage the Jian River; five stone rhinoceroses to suppress water monsters; excavated the Lidu Mountain to avoid flood disasters and channeled thirty-six rivers to irrigate the rice fields of a dozen cities and counties in southwest Sichuan. Since Yu the Great tamed the flood, Li Bing was able to follow the original course of the rivers to dredge and widen them. There is now a Li Bing Temple next to the Jianweiyan rope bridge, thirty-three *li* west of the county of Chengdu." (Quoted from *Broad Records of Shu*). Li Bing and his son, Erlang, were still clearly distinguished.

"Records of Building Sanlang Temple at the Beginning of the Yuanyou Reign" by Zhang Shangying (1043–1121) recorded: "Li Bing eliminated the floods, and the people built a temple in Sichuan to worship him. And the deity of his son Erlang changed into a saint and died in the country's service. Moved by his deeds, the emperor issued an imperial decree ordering the establishment of a temple for Erlang in Yuquan County, Hubei Province." (Cited in the *Chronicles of Xinjin County*, Daoguang Reign, Qing Dynasty). Li Bing's temple in Sichuan (specifically, on top of the Lidui, not on top of the Yubi Mountain), and Li Erlang's temple in Hubei, are not yet confused at this time.

During the Yuanfeng Reign (1078–1085) of Zhao Xu, Emperor Shenzong of the Northern Song Dynasty, Kaifeng folk repaired the shrine of Guankou Erlang and sacrificed it to Li Erlang. Gao Cheng recorded this in Volume 7, "Marquis of Ling Hui" of *Shiwu Jiyuan*: "During the Yuanfeng Reign, west of the capital Kaifeng City, the people erected the Shrine of Guankou Erlang Shen, saying that Erlang Shen was the son of Prince Guangji of Daojiang County of Yongkang Army. Prince Guangji is Li Bing of the Qin Dynasty. The titles like "second son of Li Bing" and "God Langjun" in the *Hui Yao* refer to Erlang Shen. After the Emperor's accession, he was appointed the Marquis of Ling Hui." The original text of the Song Dynasty's official revision of the "Hui Yao" is "The Shrine of God Langjun: The second son of Prince Guangyou Yinghui of Chongde Temple in Yongkang. In the eighth month of the eighth year of the Jiayou, Emperor Renzong's reign, the emperor issued a decree to especially ennoble the God Langjun from the temple of Prince Guangji of the Yongkang Army as the Marquis of Ling Hui and sent officials to offer sacrifices. God Langjun was the second son of Li Bing, and the people of Sichuan called him the King of Hu Guo Ling Ying." The emperor is Song Renzong, whose reign is also the period of the writing of the *Shiwu Jiyuan*. The name "Langjun Shrine" may be the official name of the shrine inscribed on the tablet at that time, while "Erlang Shrine" may be the common name of the people.

Zeng Zhao (1047–1107) drafted *An Edict on the Ennoblement of the Marquis of Ling Hui as the Duke of Linghui Yinggan.*

"Your father ruled Shu and built the water conservancy of the two rivers, and his merits and virtues were honored for future generations. You are also known in the west as a divine spirit. Your father and son had temples of gods that were worshipped and passed down to the present. In the second year, the people of the capital city look to you for divine blessings, and the people's difficulties, calamities, and diseases are blessed when they pray to you!" (Quoted from 择善而 从 *Ze Shan Er Cong*, the *Great Imperial Decree Collection of Song Dynasty, Xubian Zizhi Tongjian Changbian.*)

"You" is Li Erlang, the son of Li Bing, whose temple in the Northern Song Dynasty capital is probably the Shrine of God Langjun.

Li Zhi (1059–1109) created *Deyu Zhai Hua Pin* in 1098. The item of *Portrait of the Duke of Yinggan* said: "The son of Li Bing, the Governor of Shu in the Qin Dynasty, excavated the two rivers and subdued the water monster. Remembering his benevolence, the Shu people built a temple in Guankou, and he was the Erlang Shen. He was handsome and majestic and often roamed the edge of the two rivers with his slingshot, enjoying the offerings in the temple."

It is evident that at this time, the people of Guankou had enshrined Li Bing and his son in one temple.

The opening of the two rivers and the subduing of water monsters are all deeds of Li Bing and are recorded in the books of the two Han dynasties. The people of the Northern Song Dynasty generously appropriated these deeds to Li Erlang. In the Southern Song Dynasty, Zeng Minxing, Zhou Wenpu, and others renewed this confusion. Yang Wujiu then stirred up Zhao Erlang and Li Bing together again.

In year 7 of the Zhenghe Reign of Emperor Huizong of the Song Dynasty (1117), the emperor issued an imperial edict to build "Shen Bao Guan." *The Eastern Capital: A Dream of Splendor* was written in 1147 and recorded the celebration of the birthday of the Erlang Shen Shen of Guankou at Shen Bao Guan in Kaifeng, the capital of the Northern Song Dynasty. Chen Jun in the Song Dynasty, Ma Duanlin in the Yuan Dynasty, and Mr. Luo Kaiyu in the contemporary era all believe this Erlang should be Li Erlang.

In the first year of Shaoxing of Emperor Gaozong Reign (1131), the "Erlang Shrine" was set up in the official lane of Hangzhou. It seems from the exposition of the articles of Wu Zimu, Qian Shuoyou, and Zhu Xi that Li Erlang and Zhao Erlang had been confused at this time and that their perceptions were very inconsistent. And Zhou Yinghe (1213–1280) again mixed Zhao Yu and Li Bing together in the *Jingding Jiankang Zhi*.

From the records of the *History of Yuan*, as well as the Yuan poet Zhang Xian's *Eleven Songs of the Divine String · Shenglang* and other documents, Erlang Shen is still inseparable from Li Bing and involved Zhao Yu.

In the third volume of *In Search of the Sacred*, Ming Dynasty, there is an account of "Guankou Erlang Shen," stating that he was born on the 26th day of the 6th month. The full text is: "Erlang Shen Shen, named Zhao Yu, followed the Taoist priest Li Jue to live in seclusion in Qingcheng Mountain. Emperor Yang of the Sui Dynasty knew his talent and appointed him as the governor of Jiazhou. There are two rivers beside the city of Jiazhou, and an old dragon inside the river, which is specialized in doing bad things. In the spring and summer, it would cause floods to harm the people.

Zhao Yu was so angry that he led boats and led warriors and residents to beat gongs and drums along the riverbank. Zhao Yu carried a sword and jumped into the water; after a moment, the water turned red. A roar like thunder came from the edge of the stone cliff. Zhao Yu held the sword in his right hand and the dragon's head in his left and fought to jump out of the water waves. At that time, seven warriors helped Zhao Yu and became seven saints. At the end of the Sui Dynasty, the world was in turmoil. Zhao Yu abandoned his official position and went to an unknown destination. Later, when the river overflowed, the Shu people saw Zhao Yu in the mist and remembered his benevolence, so they set up a temple at Guanjiangkou to worship. Emperor Taizong of the Tang Dynasty made him the Great General of Divine Courage, Emperor Xuanzong crowned him the Prince of Chicheng, and Emperor Zhenzong of the Song Dynasty crowned him the True Lord of Qing Yuan Miao Dao." (See *Daozang*, Volume 36.)

It is also recorded in the *Chronicles of Changshu County*, Volume 3, "Rituals," during the Chongzhen period of the Ming Dynasty: "Zhao Yu resigned from his post and left; no one knew where he was going. When the water in Jiazhou was rising, people saw a man with bows and bullets, like a hunter crossing the river in the green mist. This man was Zhao Yu. Therefore, the people set up a temple in Guan River and called him Guankou Erlang Shen." At present, Zhao

Yu's hermitage is Zhao Gong Mountain in Dujiangyan.

The *Chronicles of Zunyi Prefecture* of Daoguang Reign in the Qing Dynasty said, "the Governor of Shu holding a three-pointed sword." This statement is also obviously Li Bing and Erlang Shen stirred together.

Later, during the Qing Dynasty and the Republic of China, many Guankou temples still existed outside of Guankou. This can be verified by documents such as the *Chronicles of Raozhou Prefecture* of Kangxi Reign in the Qing Dynasty, the *Jiaqing Reworking of the Daqing Yitong Zhi*, Volume 385, "The Chengdu Prefecture II," Deng Lin's *Yuxiang Zhi Lue*, Volume 8, and the Republican *Wu County Zhi*, Volume 35.

II

Liu Zongdi's article "Erlang on a White Horse from Distant Persia" (2018) also equates Li Bing with the Erlang Shen of Guankou. Liu thinks that "The story of Erlang Shen killing the dragon is indisputably in the same vein as the myth of the Persian rain god fighting the drought-bring demon." In fact, the relationship between Erlang Shen and Persia (Zoroastrianism), the *Spring and Autumn Annals of Ten Kingdoms*, Volume 37, has already hinted: "In August 920 CE, the emperor of the former Shu was dressed in golden armor, wearing a pearl cap, and leading the march with a lance and bow. Behind him, flags waved, and soldiers with weapons and armor followed the emperor's march. The whole procession was a hundred miles long. The people watched the majestic military prowess from the sidelines and could not help but sigh in admiration, praising the emperor as the Guankou Zoroastrianism God." The emperor is Wang Yan (899–926). Zhang Tangying (1029–1071) is said to be the god of Guankou.

According to Hou Hui's article "Erlang Shen: One God, Eight Divine Qualities" (2011), "Every year, on the 24th day of the 6th lunar month, which is the birthday of Erlang Shen, the people of Sichuan hold a 'Lord Chuan Fair,' with songs and dances, carrying the statue of Lord Chuan in procession. In case of drought, it is also a day to pray for rain and perform a 'rain show.' This custom has spread to various places. Shandong and Hebei will call this day the 'Rain Festival.' It is also said that this day will 'divide dragon soldiers.' If it rains, it is divided into 'diligent dragons.' Otherwise, it is a 'lazy dragon.' Therefore, the water of Erlang Shen is also the god of rain." This seems to support what Liu said.

Two examples from the Qing Dynasty cited in Li Yuanguo and Tian Miaomiao's article "On the Beliefs of the Lord Chuan and Erlang in the Bashu Region" (2012) also corroborate Liu's statement. The first example is "The people of Dayi area offer prayers to Lord Chuan on June 24 every year. If it's a drought year, they will invite the table of the Lord Chuan together and pray for the rain. If the rain prayer is fulfilled, everyone will kowtow, offer incense to Lord Chuan's tablet, and perform a play to thank the deity. And Lord Chuan is called the 'God of Rain.'" The second example is "The people of Fuling County pay homage to Li Bing, the Lord of Sichuan, on June 24. They would pray for rain whenever there was a drought year, and Li Bing would give them rain immediately."

So, Li Bing is a Chinese severe rain god.

III

It is paradoxical that *The Concordance of Science, Mythology, and Religion in China: Centering on Li Bing* (p. 259–262), "The Table of the Erlang Shrine," which elects several examples of Sichuan temples dedicated to Erlang and also to Li Bing, does not record the most important temple of Two Kings in Guan County.

According to the *Chronicles of Jiangjin County of the Qianlong Reign*, "There are temples of the gods of the Lord Chuan built in every village, township, county, and prefecture in Sichuan Province. According to the testimony, the Lord Chuan God is the god in the emperor's imperial temple of Two Kings in Dujiangyan in the present Guan County. The front temple is dedicated to Li Erlang, the son of Li Bing, the Governor of Shu in the Qin Dynasty, and the latter is dedicated to Li Bing."

According to a retired worker of a factory in Dujiangyan City, Master Xiao (born in 1949), who saw it with his own eyes and told me face to face (besides his account below, I have added my testimony and collation, some places need to be further verified), until August 1966 (there are two other accounts in September and December, to be confirmed), the Two Kings Temple in Guan County was still the central sacrifice of Erlang. Li Bing was the second. The central position in the front hall is the seated statue of the three-eyed Erlang Shen (For the photograph, see the fifth series of the *Journal of Sichuan Normal University*, 1986, *Dujiangyan Cultural Relics*, p. 100, no. 42.). The back hall is decorated with two seated statues of Li Bing and his wife (For the photograph, see the fifth series of the *Journal of Sichuan Normal University*, 1986, *Dujiangyan Cultural Relics*, p. 100, no. 41.).

IV

In the Jin Dynasty, the Shu people welcomed the statue of Li Bing into the "Fan Xian Ancestral Hall of Lidui" and worshipped it. In recognition of Li Bing's deeds of locking up the dragon, the hall was called "Fulongguan" (for details, see Ma Feibai's "Qin Ji Shi—Biography VIII").

In the Northern Song Dynasty, there was a shrine of King Du'an in Chengdu dedicated to Li Bing. Fei Zhu's *Sui Hua Ji Li Pu* states, "On the 23rd day of the first month of the lunar calendar, a silkworm market was held in front of the Shengshou Temple. The market started after Zhang Yong entered the temple, allowing the people to sell their agricultural tools. Governor Zhang Yong first worshipped the King Du'an Shrine inside the temple and then feasted." Zhang Yong paid homage to Li Bing on the 23rd day of the first month, not knowing which book of allusions the account was based on.

In the Southern Song Dynasty, during the Chunxi period, the wall of Fulongguan has a painting of Li Bing and his son by Sun Taigu. Lu You, Fan Chengda, and others can witness this. At that time, the Fulongguan was also called the "Fulong Shrine."

According to Chen Yuefang's record in the Qing Dynasty, during the Tongzhi era, the statue of Li Bing was moved to the front hall, while Erlang was placed in the back hall. This is the opposite of the layout of the Two Kings Temple.

During the Xuantong period, the front hall of Fulongguan was dedicated to the statue of Li Bing, who was crowned with his boots, with his eyes squarely on his seat and holding his imperial watts. This can be seen in the photo of the Li Bing statue at Fulongguan, which Ernst Boerschmann took in 1909.

Looking at the photo of the exterior of Fulongguan taken by Sidney David Gamble in 1917, we know that the gate and the wall of Fulongguan were no longer there during the Republican period, and the plaque of "Eternal Reliance" in the front hall can be seen clearly.

Chapter 16

Wealth Prevails: The Rise of the God of Wealth

Every year on the 24th day of the 6th lunar month, the Two Kings Temple in Dujiangyan holds a temple fair where the Taoists in the temple have a puja to celebrate the birthday of "Lord Chuan Qing Yuan Miao Dao Zhenjun" and host a Sichuan opera performance to entertain the faithful and tourists. People from all counties and towns in the western Sichuan plain flocked to the temple early in the morning from all directions to burn incense, worship, and watch the puja and Sichuan opera, making it a lively event. However, most people do not know who the god with the dual identity of Lord Chuan and Zhenjun (Taoism's honorific name for the gods) is, and they even shake their heads when asked.

The *Chronicles of Guan County*, 1991 Edition, records that the Lord Chuan puja, which takes place on the 24th day of the 6th lunar month, is said to be the birthday of Erlang. People from the city and the countryside come to the Two Kings Temple to worship. The *Chronicles of Folklore in Dujiangyan City*, 2018 Edition, adds, "In recent years, the tourism department has taken advantage of the situation and made the June 24 a 'Li Bing Cultural Festival,' making the temple fair even richer in content." If you consult the local people today, they will say: June 24 is Li Bing's birthday, and you must go to the Two Kings Temple. So, the question arises again: whose birthday is June 24th? What exactly is the relationship between Lord Chuan Qing Yuan Miao Dao Zhenjun and Li Bing?

The Story of Li Bing and Zhao Yu Killing the Dragon Is about the Apotheosis of Water Management

The old saying goes: "The holy kings set up a system of sacrifices. Those who have established great merits for the common people should be sacrificed; those who have worked hard and died in office should be sacrificed; those who have worked for the country and made it stable should be sacrificed; those who can withstand great disasters should be sacrificed; those who can deal with great calamities should be sacrificed." Li Bing, the Governor of Shu Prefecture in the Qin Dynasty, built a weir on the river, transformed floods into water conservancy, and had such deeds as ruling Shu and reviving Shu, as well as such myths as fighting rhinoceroses and defending dragons, so he was a man who could give the law to the people (the law is also merit) and could resist great disasters and defend great calamities, so he was worshipped as the "Lord Chuan" by later generations, which should be deserved. But he was not the first to be honored with the reputation of "Lord of Sichuan."

The *Chronicles of Jiangjin County* during Qianlong Regin, Volume 21, "Shu Sacrifice Lord Chuan" pointed out that the first officially certified Lord Chuan was Zhao Yu in the Sui Dynasty. According to *Tongzhi Waiji*, "Jiading Zhi Minghuan," Zhao Yu of the Sui Dynasty was a native of Qingcheng. He and the Taoist priest Li Wang traveled worldwide and repeatedly resigned from the emperor's recruitment. Later, Emperor Yang of the Sui Dynasty made him the governor of Jiazhou; when a dragon plagued the people of Jiazhou, Zhao Yu ordered the people to prepare hundreds of boats, and he led more than a thousand people to beat the drum at the river. He draped his hair and jumped into the water with a sword. Seven warriors joined him and entered the water with their hair and swords. Then there was darkness in heaven and earth. After a while, the clouds slowly dispersed, and the seven warriors did not come out; only Zhao Yu struggled out from the water. His left hand was with a sword; the right hand was carrying the dragon's head. The river water was all red, and the scourge caused by the dragon was removed. During the Kaihuang Regin, Zhao Yu led his family into the mountains to live in seclusion, and his trail was never seen again.

Later, a person transporting the court's taxes saw Zhao Yu riding a white horse, leading a white *zhang*, and a child following him with a bow and arrow on his waist. Tang Emperor Taizong named him 'General of Divine Courage' and built a temple in Guankou to worship. After Tang Emperor Xuanzong arrived in

Sichuan, Zhao Yu was crowned 'King of Chicheng.' In the Song Dynasty, when Zhang Yong ruled Sichuan, he went to the temple to pray and received help from the gods; when the chaos in Sichuan subsided and the emperor learned about it, he ennobled Zhao as 'Lord Chuan Qing Yuan Miao Dao Zhenjun.' The Lord of Sichuan, whom everyone worships now, is Zhao Yu. Some say that the Lord of Chuan is Li Bing, the Governor of Shu in the Qin Dynasty, but Li Bing has no claim to be the Lord Chuan. Such documents unanimously deny Li Bing's identity as the Lord of Sichuan.

For Zhao Yu's title, *Chronicles of Jiading Prefecture*, Volume 32 during Tongzhi Regin has a different opinion: "According to the *Book of Sui*, Jiazhou was abolished at the end of Emperor Yang's reign and was called Meishan Prefecture. By the beginning of the Tang Dynasty, it was changed back to Jiazhou. Zhao Yu served as an official of Jiazhou during the Daye period so that he would have been the governor of Meishan, not the governor of Jiazhou. The records in the *Provincial Records* and *Shen Yi Zhi* are incorrect. It was not long before Jiazhou changed its name, and it was during the Tang Dynasty, not during the Sui Dynasty." Regardless of where Zhao Yu was the governor, "Lord Chuan Qing Yuan Miao Dao Zhenjun" was his title. In retrospect, this title was specially conferred on Zhao Yu by Song Zhenzong, in compliance with the request of Zhang Yong, the governor of Yizhou.

Li Bing's ambush dragon deifies his water management behavior. Zhao Yu beheaded the dragon, which is the same. Therefore, there are descriptions of the situation, like "when the water of the Jialing River was soaring, and the Shu people missed Zhao Yu" in the *Record of Mr. Liu Longcheng* and others. From a mythological point of view, the story of Zhao Yu, the Sheriff of Jiazhou, beheading a dragon may be a "textual regeneration" of the legend of Li Bing, the Sheriff of Shu.

It is said that Zhao Yu was only twenty-six years old when he beheaded the dragon. So, when was his birthday?

Chu Renhuo, the early Qing Dynasty literary scholar, wrote in Volume 1 of *Jian Hu Ji*. "On June 24, the birth anniversary of the Qing Yuan Miao Dao Zhenjun, the Wu people must use a white rooster to worship him, a custom that has been passed down for a long time." (Note: the ancient sacrifice to Li Bing, with the sheep).

The *Chronicles of Wu County*, Volume 35, during the Republic of China Era, recorded that the Qing Yuan Miao Dao Zhenjun Temple in Wu County, Jiangsu

Province, is dedicated to the god Zhao Yu, and note that the temple is commonly known as the Temple of Gunakou Erlang Shen, it is said that June 24 is the birth of the god. Meanwhile, many chronicles have approved that God Zhao Yu is from Guanzhou, and June 24 is his birthday. All men and women in the city go to the temple on this day to worship and pray for the blessing of god. In the eyes of the Wu people, Zhao Yu was not only the Qing Yuan Miao Dao Zhenjun but also the "God of Guankou Erlang," and because "when people prayed for their illnesses, they were always answered" (the sick were cured, that is, they were answered), which was a bit like the Bodhisattva of Medicine, so it was widely believed in Wu, not only in Shu.

On the Misunderstanding of Li Bing and Zhao Yu's Faith

The most famous temple of Qing Yuan Miao Dao Zhenjun outside of Sichuan is the "Erlang Temple" built by Emperor Song Gaozong in the first year of the Shaoxing Regin (1131). According to Wu Zimu's *Meng Liang Lu*, Volume 14, "Dongdu Sui Chao Ancestral Hall," "the Temple of Erlang Shen, the Qing Yuan Dao Jiao Zhenjun, was built in Official Lane during the Shaoxing Reign. *The Old History* mentioned that the shrine was built in Kaifeng. With the relocation of the Southern Song Dynasty to Hangzhou, the temple was established there as well." This Erlang is Zhao Erlang or Zhao Yu, whose ancestral shrine is in the middle section of Imperial Street in the capital city of the Southern Song Dynasty, Lin'an Prefecture (Hangzhou), in Guanxiang. Shou'an Square was formerly known as "Guanxiang," commonly called "Guanxiang." According to the old records, a shrine in Bianliang City (Kaifeng) in the Northern Song Dynasty was moved to Hangzhou in the Southern Song Dynasty.

Qing Yuan Miao Dao Zhenjun can be shortened to "Qing Yuan Zhenjun" or "Qing Yuan." The Song Dynasty lyricist and calligrapher Yang Wujiu (1097–1171) had a poem, "Erlang Shen (the birth anniversary of Qingyuan)" in his "Escape from Zen Lyrics." One sentence is: "Erlang Shen caught the evil dragon in Guankou and pacified the flooding in Lidui." Intentionally or unintentionally, Zhao Yu and Li Bing were stirred together.

In the Yuan Dynasty, someone composed *A Poem on Qing Yuan Zhenjun June 24 Birth Anniversary*, praise also Zhao Yu's achievements and magical powers. The *Chronicles of Shifang County* during the Republic of China Era also mixed Zhao Yu, Li Bing, and Li Bing's son Li Erlang. The events have been entangled.

Zhao Yu's birth date was grafted onto Li Bing, or Li Erlang, which is unsurprising.

In the Qing Dynasty, knowledgeable people could distinguish between Li Bing, Li Erlang, and Zhao Yu. Wang Pei Xun recorded in *Ting Yu Lou Sui Bi*, Volume 4: "There are temples of Lord Chuan in various counties in Sichuan Province, and some people believe that Lord Chuan is the god of Guankou Erlang. Erlang, the son of Li Bing, a Qin governor, was credited with helping his father rule water. Li Bing had his own shrine in Guankou, next to the temple of Lord Chuan, which locals' thought was the temple of Li Erlang. Across from the temple is Zhao Gong Mountain. According to the record that Zhao Yu beheaded the dragon in Jiazhou in the Sui Dynasty, there is also a theory that the dragon was beheaded in Jianwei. The Song Dynasty named Zhao Yu as the True Lord of Chuan Qing Yuan, so the Lord Chuan should be Zhao Yu. He lived in seclusion on Mount Zhaogong, so a shrine was built in Guankou. During the Song Dynasty, Erlang Temple was very prosperous. It is wrong to confuse these together, and most learned people can distinguish them." Obviously, Wang Peixun (1783–1859) saw the same pattern as today's Two Kings Temple: the temple of Erlang (Lord Chuan Temple) and Li Bing Temple have been combined into one, Erlang in the front hall, Li Bing in the back hall.

Two Kings Temple and Mount Zhaogong Were Zhao Yu's Dojo

The place where Zhao Yu was worshipped in Shu, the Dragon God Shrine, in Leshan City, still exists today. Recently, the shrine was a newly sculpted bronze statue of Zhao Yu, still holding a sword and the appearance of the wave out. In fact, according to the "Birthday of Lord Chuan Qing Yuan Miao Dao Zhenjun," it can be deduced that the Erlang Shen in the front hall of the Two Kings Temple should also be the statue of Zhao Yu. Only later, statue makers were influenced by novels such as *The Legend of the Gods* and *Journey to the West*, as well as operas such as *Saving the mother on the Splitting Mountain*, so they mistakenly portrayed Erlang Shen as Yang Jian.

Why do you say this? It can be seen from the alternative treatment of the front hall of the Two Kings Temple in the Qing Dynasty.

A three-tipped, two-edged sword, about 3 meters high and made of iron, stood on the left side of the cloister outside the temple. In contrast, a snarling dog, also made of iron, stood on the right side, also cast by the Taoist priest Wang Laitong at the beginning of the Qianlong period. It is well known that the three-pointed sword and the snarling dog were the standard accessories for Yang Jian, who had three eyes on his face. Zhao Yu, however, was once the Erlang Shen from Guankou, who was no longer known to the Daoist priest Wang.

However, why was Zhao Yu called Erlang? The answer is hidden in Mr. Liu's *Dragon City Records* under the title *Zhao Yu Zhan Jiao*: "Zhao Yu styled himself Zhongming, and his brother Zhao Mian are hidden in Mount Qingcheng." Zhao Yu's style name is Zhongming. Zhong means the second in line. He has a brother named Zhao Mian, the so-called Erlang. Although Mr. Liu's *Dragon City Records* was signed under the name of Liu Zongyuan (written by Wang Zhi, a Song scholar, and assumed Liu's name), it was not a famous work after all, and Daoist Wang probably had not read it.

The opposite bank of the Two Kings Temple is Damian Mountain. Because of Zhao Yu, the mountain is also named Zhao Gong Mountain. The so-called "and brother Mian all hidden Qingcheng Mountain" is said on a wide range, specifically in Mount Zhaogong. This is like the local, Dujiangyan is a separate city, but to the outside world, Dujiangyan is only a part of Chengdu. The Yulei Mountain, where the Two Kings Temple is located, is situated in the Ling Yan Mountain (there is the "Happy Rain Place," which was completed in the 21st year of the Jiaqing period, with the words "Fifth Cave Heaven" inscribed on it. The fifth cave is the ranking name of Qingcheng Mountain in the Taoist system), but people in the Qing Dynasty called it "the Yulei of Qingcheng." Mount Zhaogong, next to Qingcheng Mountain, is also part of the "800 miles of Qingcheng." If we look at the contemporary administrative division, what the ancients called Qingcheng Mountain spans the adjacent areas of Dujiangyan, Chongzhou, Dayi, and Wenchuan counties, so it can be called the "vast educational master" among the mountains in the southwest.

Perhaps the confusion between "Zhao Zhongming" and "Zhao Gongming" now has led to official propaganda: Mount Zhaogong is Zhao Gongming's retreat place, and it is the god of wealth in Chengdu. Unbeknownst to us, the ancient people all agreed that Mount Zhaogong was the mountain where Zhao Yu lived in seclusion.

Qingcheng and Guanzhou (Guanzhou, Guan County, and Guankou are the old names of the city of Dujiangyan). In today's words, Zhao Yu is a native of Dujiangyan. But paradoxically, the entire area of Dujiangyan today is no place for Zhao Yu to land. Two Kings Temple and Mount Zhaogong were once his dojos. Still, they are all collectively forgotten, except for the temple's name, and the banners hung at the annual festival occasionally make people think. Many historical details, just like the Yubi floating clouds, look to sail away without a trace.

What could be the deeper reasons for Zhao Yu being forgotten? Perhaps as the first year of the Guangxu Reign engraved the *Chronicles of Pengshui County* analysis: "It has been proved that both Zhao Yu and Li Bing were called the Lord of Sichuan because they both made outstanding achievements for Sichuan by ruling water. However, Li Bing became the lord of Sichuan before Zhao Yu. Moreover, Li Bing ruled the entire upper reaches of Sichuan, while Zhao Yu was only in Jiazhou. Li Bing plucked open the riverbank and built Dujiangyan, which made great achievements for the people. In particular, he could remove harm and raise profit and was known for more than just miraculous deeds. Like Zhao Yu beheaded the demon dragon, only by the Taoist magical powers to block a momentary disaster cannot make the people a thousand years later can still enjoy the benefits. So, after discussion, the court settled on giving Li Bing the title of King of Fuze Xingji Tongyou and Erlang, the title of King of Chengji Guanghui Xianying. And Zhao Yu's title was added by past dynasties and was not agreed upon by the current dynasty, so the power of the guest and the host is clear at a glance." The *Chronicles of Qianjiang County* has the same writing. This is a bit of a suspicion that the size of the credit judges the hero, but it can be seen as an argument.

Fig. 2 Bronze statue of Zhao Yu at the Dragon God Shrine in Leshan.
Photo by Li Chengzhi.

CHAPTER 17

———— ✦✦✦ ————

The "Land of Abundance" in the Han Portraits

When visiting museums and famous monuments in Sichuan or viewing calligraphic inscriptions, you can inadvertently see several high-frequency words appearing back and forth: "fertile land," "fertile field of thousands miles," "natural abundance," "land of abundance," "field of abundance." They are now synonymous with Sichuan or the Chengdu Plain, and they are the mantra of the Sichuan people, always full of pride when they are spoken and written.

Tianfu: Shifting from Guanzhong Plain to Chengdu Plain

Before the capital of the Western Han Dynasty was established, the terms "fertile field of thousands miles" and "land of abundance" were used to refer to the area ruled by the Qin Dynasty, especially the Guanzhong Plain. *The Warring States Strategy*, a national history book, describes the State of Qin in the name of the famous diplomat Su Qin: "The west has the advantages of Ba, Shu, and Hanzhong, the north has the use of Hu raccoon and Dai horse, the south has the limit of Wushan and Qianzhong, and the east has the solidity of Xiao and Han. The fields are fertile, the people are rich, and they can send out ten-thousand chariots, a million armies, a thousand miles of fertile land, rich in products, and the terrain is convenient. This is Tianfu, the most powerful country in the world."

In the late Qin and early Han dynasties, Liu Bang's adviser Zhang Liang made a retelling of the same meaning: "The left of Guanzhong is Xiaohan, the right is Long and Shu. Fertile fields for thousands of miles, the south has the rich Bashu, and the north has the advantage of Hu Yuan … this so-called gold city of a thousand miles, the country of heaven as well."

Until Zhang Liang died more than a hundred years later, "a thousand miles of fertile land" began to be borrowed by the Shu people to describe the Shu, especially the Chengdu plain. Yang Xiong, a native of Chengdu, known as the "Confucius of the Western Road," wrote in his fiction: "The land of the capital of Shu was called Liangzhou in ancient times. When Yu the Great was here to govern the river, he used to observe the riverside. There were dense forests everywhere and fertile fields for thousands of miles." After the success of Yu's water treatment, the world was divided into nine states, of which Liangzhou corresponds to Shu. Looking at it today, Shu is a land with a dense network of water, rich land, and lush vegetation, which can be called "fertile fields for a thousand miles." The word "沃 fertile" means irrigated. It is said that the land has the benefit of irrigation, so it is called fertile land. Of course, several decades earlier than Yang Xiong, the Guanzhong historian Sima Qian praised Sichuan and Chengdu Plain with the word "fertile field." The main reason why Shu became fertile is the benefit of Dujiangyan irrigation, just as the main reason why Guanzhong Plain became fertile is the use of Zhengguo Canal irrigation.

In the fifth year of the Yuanfeng Reign (106 BCE), Emperor Wu of the Han Dynasty changed the name of "Liangzhou" to "Yizhou." About why Shu could replace Guanzhong and become a new fertile land, Qin Mi, a bachelor of Yizhou, had his analysis: "In Shu, there is the mountain of Wenfu, from which the Min River flows. When you are an emperor here, the country prospers; and the gods will give blessings. So, this place is fertile for a thousand miles." It is very vague, but the benefit of the river (the Min River, on which the Dujiangyan was built) water is still one of its roots.

In the Rites of Zhou, "Tianfu" means national treasury, "All jade, bronze and other important treasures of the country are collected in the national treasury." Zhuangzi uses the term "Tianfu" to describe a realm: "Fill the wine is never full, pour the wine is never finished." Later generations praised this rich and well-endowed land, also known as Tianfu. The earliest person who used the term

"Tianfu" and "a fertile land of a thousand miles" to praise Shu was Zhuge Liang, Liu Bei's adviser, who said, "Yizhou has a treacherous frontier, a fertile wilderness of a thousand miles, and the land of the Heavenly Palace, where Emperor Gaozu achieved his empire." Gaozu is Liu Bang. This statement by Zhuge Liang only moved the scope of what Zhang Liang said from the Guanzhong Plain to the Chengdu Plain.

So, who will prove that Sima Qian, Yang Xiong, Qin Mi, and Zhuge Liang are true to their words? Or, to put it differently, is there any non-written source other than the words of these famous people that can show that Sichuan was the new Land of Abundance?

History is like a cloud of smoke that passes by, but fortunately, some texts and images can be used to preserve its essence. They are buried deep in the ground, sealed in ancient scrolls, or sometimes in the form of indecipherable remnants on the roads and roadsides where people often pass, waiting to be unearthed,

The portrait bricks and stones are historical carriers primarily buried in the strata, echoing and complementing each other in the form of images, illustrations, and literature.

The bricks and stones with portraits mainly decorated in tombs and shrines during the Han Dynasty are called "Han portrait bricks" and "Han portrait stones." Han portrait bricks are primarily found in Henan and Sichuan provinces, with a few in Shandong, Shaanxi, Jiangsu, Hubei, Jiangxi, Yunnan, and other places. Han portrait stones are primarily found in western and southern Shandong, northern Jiangsu, the Minjiang region in west Sichuan, Nanyang in Henan, Suide in Shaanxi, and Luliang in Shanxi.

Han portrait bricks and Han portrait stones have a wide range of subjects and rich contents. Their lifelike, vivid, dynamic, and unparalleled artistic expression techniques vividly and concretely demonstrate the richness and profundity of Han culture, just like the photographic images of the time, supplementing the shortage of written records and changing the plane into a three-dimensional one, which is a valuable physical material for studying the society, customs, and literature of the two Han dynasties and has a unique history. It has a special historical status and a high heritage value.

Combing through the Han portrait bricks and Han portrait stones unearthed in Sichuan over the years, we will be surprised to find that many of them can be used as framed visual materials to support the theories of Sima Qian, Yang Xiong, Qin Mi, Zhuge Liang, and others about the fertile land of the heaven.

Shooting and Harvest Portrait Brick in the Han Dynasty

In year 6 of the Yuanding Reign (111 BCE), Sima Qian was ordered by Emperor Wu of the Han Dynasty to go to Ba, Shu, and Yunnan, which was an essential part of the Han Dynasty's primary policy for the southwest. Before that, Tang Meng, the general of the Han Dynasty, had been working hard to build the "Southwest Yi Road," which had caused "great panic among the people of Ba and Shu" and was about to mutiny. Sima Xiangru, a native of Chengdu, was ordered to go there, and it took some written instructions and oral pacification to stabilize the situation. At the same time, the chiefs of Qiong and Zha (around Xichang and Hanyuan in Sichuan) also submitted to the Han Dynasty. Nineteen years later, Sima Qian went further than his predecessors, not only to the south of Bashu but also to Kunming, the hinterland of central Yunnan (which was more significant than the present Kunming area). This year, the Han Dynasty established the five prefectures of Zangke, Yuexi, Shenli, Wenshan, and Wudu. At this point, the operation of the southwest was considered more concrete and ended. The harvest of Sima Qian's work was not only in terms of the state but also in terms of literature, such as the "Biography of the Southwest Barbarians" and the "Biography of the Goods and Services," which are very charming geographical essays.

In the "Biography of the Goods and Services," Sima Qian recalled: "The Guanzhong region starts from the west of Qian County and Yong County, east to the Yellow River and Huashan Mountain, which has a fertile field for thousands of miles. Bashu also has a vast fertile land and is rich in goblets, ginger, tans, stone, copper, iron, and utensils made of bamboo and wood. The southern part of Bashu was connected to the Bo Road of the Yunnan-Yue Kingdom, where the population of the Bo tribe was taken and sold. Bashu was also connected to Qiongdu and Zuodu in the west, so people were selling Zuo horses and yaks to and from Bashu. Although there are mountains on all sides, thousands of miles of trestle roads in the mountains are accessible in all directions. Only the Baoxie Road controls the exit of Bashu to the north, and through this road, Bashu people exchange what they need with what they have in excess." Like many ancient people, Sima Qian also entered Shu from the Baoxie Road. Although Shu is the land of four plugs, and the Shu Road is complicated to walk, the stack road connects thousands of miles, materials, and culture to the outside world and is also unstoppable. The ancient Shu period, represented by the Sanxingdui site and Jinsha site as a civilization, has had a variety of exchanges with the outside world, not to mention the prosperity and openness of the Western Han Dynasty "five capitals," (Luoyang, Handan, Linzi, Wan, Chengdu) period.

Although Ban Gu, the historian of the Eastern Han Dynasty, did not set foot in Shuzhong, he continued the central theme of sunshine set by Sima Qian in the *Book of Han · Treatise on Geography*. He said: "The land of Shu Prefecture is fertile, with ample river water, fertile fields, dense mountains, and forests, bamboo and wood, vegetable food and fruits in abundance ... The people eat rice and fish and forget about the worries of disaster years."

There is a square portrait brick (see Fig. 3), named by archaeologists as the "Shooting and Harvest Portrait Brick," which can be taken as a visual illustration and artistic expression of this passage of Ban Gu.

The brick was molded and fired, and some were painted with color. Because they were mass-produced, they frequently appeared in different locations and tombs in Sichuan while maintaining the same portrait. For example, brick chamber tombs No. 1, No. 2, and No. 10 in Yangzi Mountain, Chengdu, all have inlays. Their dimensions are small, being around 40 cm in height and width.

The brick is divided into two, the upper part wide and the lower part narrow, independent of each other, but also as one, with the feeling of a separate screen for film and television. The upper part can be regarded as "Shooting": in the autumn month, the grass and trees are yellow and fallen, and on the edge of the countryside, there are two men (perhaps they are both *cifei*, Han Dynasty military officials who are in charge of the shooting) in military attire (the style seems to be similar to that of the warriors in the Jinqueshan Han tomb in Linyi, Shandong), opening their bows to shoot geese (But no arrow or that has been shot, maybe for the sake of the picture and deliberately left white not painted), *Fei* (*Zengzuo* Machine) with a long and thin rope tied to the ground is attached to the arrow (left with a perforation); the second half can be regarded as the "Harvest Rice Picture." In the middle of the southern mu, three peasants wearing buns and shin cloths bow down and take the sickle to pinch the ears. At the same time, the other two raise their arms and wield the skull to mow and remove the grain and grass that has been removed from the ears, and on the leftmost side is a messenger, who is ready to return after the meal, carrying the equipment and the bundle of rice on his shoulder.

The two images are combined to show that it is the time of another year's harvest, with flying geese in the sky, floating eiders in the water, carp playing with lotuses, and fragrant rice fields, a vivid scene of the Land of Abundance. One can't help but think of the chanting in the *Classic of Poetry*:

> The geese are flying in the sky with their beautiful feathers.
> Let's take out short arrows and shoot geese.
> We got rice in October, so we can use this to make spring wine.
> I will drink with you, dear one, and grow old with you.

However, if the word "rice" is replaced by "silk reeling," the mood created in the poems of Tang and Song might be even more apt.

LEFT Fig. 3 Topography of "Shooting and Harvest Brick" from the Han tomb at Yangzi Mountain, Chengdu, Sichuan.

BELOW Fig. 4 "Freshwater Farming Pictorial Stone" excavated in Guan County, Sichuan. Provided by Fu Sanyun.

The wild yard lists a few spring rocks.

The thorny casement backs the beautiful village.

In the early winter, I was in my leisure time farming.

I shot down a flock of geese and cooked a fish.

The soup is fresh because of the new geese.

The jacket is lightly warmed by silk reeling.

The farming family is happy at the end of the year.

These officials may not know this kind of joy.

Suppose the "Shooting Goose Picture" of the "Shooting and Harvest Brick" shows a pond in the wild of Chengdu Plain, which is still relatively original. In that case, the "Freshwater Farming Picture Stone" (from now on also called "Stone Carving Water Pond," See Fig. 4), which was unearthed in 1964 in Guan County (present-day Dujiangyan City) and is now displayed in Fulongguan, a scenic area of Dujiangyan, is a miniature depiction of the basic appearance of an artificial pond in Chengdu during the Han Dynasty, which is very typical. The pond is called "Fishpond" in the words of the *Records of the Grand Historian*.

The stone pond is 151 cm long, 85.2 cm wide, and 17 cm thick and is divided into three parts in a jigsaw puzzle: a tree, a boat, and three bunches of seedling dough are carved in the rice paddy on the left, during which eight people bend over to work, while a woman holding a parasol watches with her baby in her arms; five lotus puffs, three snails, two frogs, and three ducks are carved in the upper half of the pond on the right, and there is a flush sluice gate and a trapezoidal water fence. Wang Bao, a rhetorician of Shu Prefecture in the Western Han Dynasty, said in the *Boy's Testament*: "In the back garden, there are more than a hundred geese and rustlers." In the lower half of the pond on the right, two lotus leaves, one crab, one turtle, and five fish are carved, and there is also a flat sluice gate and a triangular water fence each. Although the shapes of the two water fences are different, they are designed to prevent various aquatic products from slipping away or running away when the water gate is released. The two vertical and horizontal borders separating the left and right areas can be regarded as the ridge of the field.

Chronicles of Huayang has described the Chengdu plain after Li Bing constructed the Dujiangyan: "Li Bing then blocked the river for the diversion dike, through the Pi River and Jian River, other tributaries along the two rivers flowing through Chengdu, the boats can be used. Minshan produces a lot of catalpas, cypress, and bamboo; these trees along the water left, sitting on the shore, can save effort and also produce a wealth of products. Li Bing also built a new water conservancy to irrigate the three counties and open rice fields widely. As a result, the fertile fields of Shu were called the 'land sea.' In the dry season, water was diverted for irrigation, and in the rainy season, the gates were closed. Therefore, it is written: "The people of Chengdu did not know what famine was, and they never had a bad year. Chengdu has been known as Tianfu ever since." The sluice gate in the stone pond may differ in size from the so-called "water gate" here. Still, it also controls the flow and regulates the water level: when planting rice, the sluice gate will be closed to let the water moisten the seedlings; during the tillering period, the sluice gate will be opened to drain the sunny field. The Freshwater Aquaculture Pictorial Stone uses a boat to symbolize the time when the rice planting field is storing water and an umbrella to indicate the time when it is exposed to the sun in the dry season, which is very clever.

Chronicles of Huayang also stated: "The soil needed to build the city of Chengdu came from a place ten miles outside the city. The large pits were used to raise fish, creating the current Wansui Pond. To the north of Chengdu, there is Longba Pond. To the east of the city, there is Qianqiu Pond; to the west, there is Liu Pond; to the northwest, there is Tianjing Pond. The water flow between each pool is directly connected, and winter and summer are not dried up. Along these ponds, a variety of garden beds were built." All sides outside Chengdu are pools. They are connected to the aqueduct, and winter and summer water flow is inexhaustible; people raise seasonal fish in it; the gardens are built next to the pools, you can cultivate trees, and so on. In this way, the cycle is repeated, the industrial chain is formed, and the economy and ecology are sustainable development. Stone carving of the pond, the same can be achieved, "freshwater aquaculture portrait stone" on the tree that is a symbol of the garden catch.

Eating and Playing in Sichuan, the Story since the Ancient Times

When people return from outdoor farming and harvesting, they must again be busy with their mouths. Going through the hall and into the kitchen must be repeated several times daily.

The Sichuan Provincial Museum has two "kitchen bricks" unearthed in Pengzhou, which are so rich in smoke and fire that they allow us to travel back a thousand years to get a glimpse of the kitchen, the interior layout, and the architectural features of the Han Dynasty.

On one side (see Fig. 5 for its topography), two gables symbolize the four-sided slope of the curved eaves roof, the "Si'e Hip Roof." Roofs are the most representative part of classical Chinese architecture. There are many roofs in the unearthed Han Dynasty architectural vessels, including Chinese Gabled Roofs, Two-slope Gabled Roofs, Xieshan Gable and Hip Roofs, Pyramidal Roofs, and Si'e Hip Roofs; almost all the roof forms used in the Ming and Qing dynasties have appeared. Among them, the Si'e Hip Roofs and Gabled Roofs are the most common, with the former draining on four sides and the latter on two sides.

On the left are two people sitting on their knees behind a long table, preparing dishes, and behind them, there is a wooden rack with three pieces of raw meat hanging. On the right side is a rectangular stove with a kettle and a retort, and a man standing in front of the stove, reaching out to operate the response. In recent years, several ceramic stove models have been unearthed in Han tombs in Sichuan, identical to the stove in the portrait.

On the other side (see Fig. 6), the roof is omitted, and the kitchen is directly close-up. On the left, two people sit on the floor behind a long table, holding knives and cutting food, talking while they do so, with two elbows and a piece of raw meat hanging on a tripod behind them. On the right is a large kettle on a tripod with wood burning under it and a man sitting on his knees in front of it, shaking his fan to help the fire. A little farther away, there are four overlapping food cases on which bowls, plates, and other tableware are neatly arranged.

Since Dujiangyan was a constant source of nourishment, Chengdu was the first to enter a new era of "The people of Chengdu did not know what famine was, and they never had a bad year." And the whole plain soon became a fertile field. The *Classic Mountains and Seas* mention the terms like Gaoshu, Gaodao, Gaosu, and Gaoji, which means delicious and creamy beans, rice, millet, and sorghum. The *Records of the Grand Historian* records *dunchi*, extra-large taro, a staple food, and miscellaneous food produced in the Warring States period. The people of Chengdu during the two Han dynasties were, of course, as industrious as ever, and that's how they came to have bamboo, vegetables, fruits, fish, and meat, the box of "grains and kernels" that was unearthed in the Han tomb at Fenghuang Mountain in Chengdu, the rice, fish, and wild eider on the "Shooting and Harvest Portrait Brick," the chickens, ducks and animals on the portrait stones of the Han tomb in Zengjiabao, Chengdu, and the pork on the "kitchen portrait brick" from

Fig. 5 The Western Han Dynasty's Kitchen Brick was unearthed in Pengzhou, Sichuan Provincial Museum.

Fig. 6 The Western Han Dynasty's Kitchen Brick was unearthed in Pengzhou, Sichuan Provincial Museum.

Pengzhou is the best and most vivid depiction and proof.

After the food is complete, they know the honor and shame and understand the etiquette, and the Chengdu people will begin to engage in recreational activities. One of the most important is to drive a horse and carriage out of the city, and this habit has continued to this day.

As for what horse and what car, *Chronicles of Huayang* has sporadic records: Ten miles north of Chengdu City, there is a Shengxian Bridge and Songke Temple.

Sima Xiangru first went to Chang'an and had inscribed on the city gate: 'If I do not ride on a high horse in a luxury vehicle, I will never walk from under this city gate.' So, many bridges were built on the river, and most blocks in Sichuan were named after the bridges. The Han Dynasty nobleman only used the red carriage. The *Book of the Later Han · Treatise on the Xianbei* records: "Empress Dowager Deng gave King Yan Liyang the seal and ribbon and three red carriages." The carriage was driven by a team of horses, which means it was big and luxurious. Today, the Sima Bridge in the north of Chengdu is just borrowed from Sima Xiangru's famous oath of struggle to name it, and the Shengxian Bridge has long since gone up in smoke. It can only be imitated in the portraits on the excavated Han bricks.

The "portrait brick of a carriage and horse crossing a bridge" in the Sichuan Museum (see Figs. 7 and 8) was unearthed in 1956 at the Tiaocheng River in Chengdu, 45.5 cm long, 40 cm wide, and 6 cm thick. The bottom of the picture is a flat wooden bridge with railings; the bridge plate is laid horizontally and vertically, under which there are four rows of bridge pillars, four pillars per row. The left end of the bridge is slightly sloped, with two horses pulling a covered light carriage galloping across the bridge. The car carries two passengers. The right person is the driver, the left is an official, and a rider behind the vehicle is closely followed. From the car system and riding point of view, the car is not the general guide car; it should be the main car. This brick depicts all the structures of the Han Dynasty beam and pillar bridges, providing valuable pictorial data and physical examples for studying ancient bridge architecture in the Han Dynasty.

The Yao carriage was the most common small vehicle of the Han Dynasty. The Yao carriage was also known as a remote car, meaning it could look far in four directions, from the front to the back, from left to right. The Yao carriage was an open carriage with no cloth on all sides to cover it, and the interior space was relatively small. The *Book of Han* says that Wang Mang had a giant named "Ju Wu Ba" who was so tall that "the Yao carriage could not carry, and three horses could not win." The only way to carry him was to use a "big carriage with four horses," like a red carriage. Because of the small carriage, the car was fast, so the Yao carriage was also called a "light car," and often drove only one horse to gallop like the wind.

In addition to driving, people in Chengdu during the Han Dynasty were also good at driving boats. Yang Xiong's *Shu Capital Rhapsody* described it colorfully: "When spring is ushered in, and the waxing moon is sent away, families with a

Fig. 7 "Carriage and Horse Crossing the Bridge" in the Sichuan Museum, Eastern Han Dynasty.

Fig. 8 Topograph of "Carriage and Horse Crossing Bridge" in Chongqing Sanxia Museum.

hundred gold pieces and a thousand gold pieces sail their boats on the river to see the fish in the river."

Not only this, but they also had other "auspicious days and festivals" to drink and make merry: "Set up wine inside a villa by the water. Feast inside the high halls of prosperous Chengdu." Set up a seat and wine in the leisure house by the water and luxurious lofty hall, and this is an indoor party. "Extending the curtain and raising the curtain, connecting the tent with the grange" is an outdoor picnic. Specifically, the curtain is a kind of "step barrier" used to enclose the space; its specific image is seen in the ancient portrait stone tomb in Yinan, Shandong Province, a piece of the Eastern Han Dynasty portrait stone (see Fig. 9). It was tied to the ground column, pulling the rope at the head of the column, hanging under the curtain made. It can be used in the courtyard and countryside to block wind and dust and protect privacy, and it is convenient to build, string, and

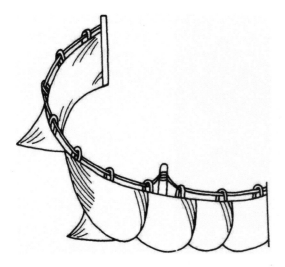

Fig. 9 "Step Barrier" on the portrait stone in Yinan, Shandong.

dismantle, so it was quite popular in the Wei-Jin and North-South dynasties. Mr. Sun Ji, a famous contemporary scholar, has traced its origin and believes that "it was already there in the Eastern Han Dynasty." Today, after reading Yang Xiong's *Shu Capital Rhapsody*, we can see that such facilities were already available in Sichuan during the Western Han Dynasty.

Besides the delicious food and wine, there were also fiddling and drumming, singing and dancing, and juggling performances, just like the family banquet of Zhuo Wenjun's family, which was vivacious. At that time, playing mahjong was unpopular, and people liked to "hit the *bo*."

Bo is six *bo*, also known as *lubo*, a very popular game during the two Han dynasties, mainly by throwing six "*bo*" (also known as *zhu*, arrow, *jiu*, etc., long strips, usually made of bamboo, with a crescent-shaped cross section) to determine the number of moves, in a specific game of chess "Bo Board" on the line to win. There is also direct dice throwing (called *qiong*), but only in kind, and the Han tomb portraits show many *lubo* with six *bo*. The subject of the "*lubo*" game is prevalent in the images of Han tombs in Sichuan (see Fig. 10), where there are both regular and immortal players. There are two types of *bo* games, one of which is not unlike those found in other regions; the other is currently found only in Sichuan and is more popular than the former, as it appears in the scene of the immortal's six *bo*. Some experts named the latter "hook rope and *bo* bureau," which is a direct reflection of the most basic cosmic pattern in the conception of the people of the time. The Shu people at that time designed this kind of *bo*

Fig. 10 The Six Bo Figures of Immortals on the Han Painting Stone in Xinjin, Sichuan.

bureau for the immortals, and the immortals played on it, directly reflecting the philosophical and religious meaning of running the universe with the six lines of *yin* and *yang* and expressing the idea of ascending to immortality with heaven and earth and traveling with the creation.

Zengjiabao Han tomb, besides the portrait stone, also unearthed three Eastern Han portrait bricks at the same time. They are, respectively, "song and dance banquet music portrait brick," "song and dance acrobatics portrait brick," and "six Bo portrait brick" (other Han tombs also found similar bricks), which not only gives us a glimpse of the peaceful life in Chengdu at that time but also opens the eyes of outsiders: the original Chengdu people can play and have fun, which is quite a tradition.

CHAPTER 18

The Detailed Explanation of "Shooting and Harvest Portrait Brick"

The "Shooting and Harvest Portrait Brick (see Fig. 11)," also known as the "Harvest Fishing and Hunting Portrait Brick," was excavated in 1954 from No. 2 Han tomb in Yangzi Mountain, Chengdu, and the brick is 45.8 cm high and 40 cm wide. It is so representative that it was printed as a unique stamp in 1956 and included in various textbooks.

The specific content of the portrait is explained on the website of the National Museum of China (by Wang Yonghong. Starting now referred to as "Wang's text") as follows.

> This brick portrait comprises two parts: The upper part is a portrait of *yi* shooting, in which two *yi* shooters are shooting with their bows, and the short arrows they use are tied with a thread, the other end of which is attached to a *bo*, and the *bo* is placed in a semicircular machine; the lake is covered with lotus leaves, the lotus flowers are fragrant, the fish and ducks are swimming, and the flying geese are in the air. The *yi* shooting refers to the activity of shooting birds by tying the arrows with silk strands. The short arrows used by the shooters were called *zeng*, the silk strands were called *jiao*, and the other end was tied with a *bo* that could slide. The *bo* in the picture is housed in a kind of semi-circular machine.

Fig. 11 The Shooting and Harvest Portrait Brick, also known as the Harvest Fishing and Hunting Portrait Brick. Now it is collected by the National Museum of China.

The picture below shows the harvest. It depicts the scene of carrying the bundle of rice on the shoulder, pinching the ears with the hand scythe, and mowing the stalks with the skull scythe. On the left, the three cutters use the hand scythe with one hand, while on the right, the two cutters use the large scythe to remove the stalks. This brick shows the production of agriculture, fishing, and hunting at that time.

The harvesting tools of the Han Dynasty were sickles and scythes. The sickle was used to pinch the ears of the grain; the instrument used in the above harvest picture is equivalent to the modern claw sickle. The wooden handle of the banner was a more advanced tool during the Han Dynasty, and it had a wide mowing area and high efficiency. A physical object was excavated from the Han tomb at Mumashan, Xinjin, Sichuan, and is like the wooden scythe in the harvest image.

In addition, Liu Zhiyuan, Shen Congwen, Sun Ji, and others also have different interpretations of the portraits, among which Liu's article "The Social

Life Reflected in the Portrait Bricks of the Han Dynasty in Sichuan" ("Liu's article") is the most concise.

> The "Yi Shooting" and "Harvesting" bricks vividly reflect the rural scene in Shu. It is the harvest season in autumn, with geese flying in the sky, lotus blossoms in the pond, and rice ears in the field. In the upper part of the lotus pond, the green leaves cover the pond, the flowers are dense, and the water ducks and fish swim among them. Two Yi shooters hid in the shade of the pond bank and shot with the arrows. A toolbox was placed beside each of the two men to collect the ropes. The lower half is a picture of rice harvesting, with three people in the middle bending over to harvest the ears of grain and two on the right holding hooks to mow the grain and grass. One person on the left carries a basket in one hand and collects a load of tied ears of grain on his shoulder. Rice harvesting in Shu was done by cutting the ears of the grain first and then mowing the grass.

First, let us discuss Chinese characters. The word 磻 (bo) is found in *Explaining Simple and Analyzing Compound Characters*, which means "to shoot with a stone tied to an arrow." To prevent the birds from fleeing with their yarns, a round stone was attached to the end of the rope, and this stone is *bo* (its image is shown in the image of a Warring States hunting bronze pot excavated in Liulige, Hui County, Henan Province). The word 钹 (po) is found in *Explaining Simple and Analyzing Compound Characters*. It means "a long, curved sickle with two edges and a wooden handle for mowing grass." The word 铚 (zhi) is also found in *Explaining Simple and Analyzing Compound Characters*, which means "short sickle for harvesting." The character 籪 (yan), also found in *Explaining Simple and Analyzing Compound Characters*, means "camouflage for archery"; the object used to hide the shooter is 籪. The character 箙, which can be found in *Explaining Simple and Analyzing Compound Characters*, has three pronunciations: *Fei, Ba,* and *Fa* (*Fei* is in *Explaining Simple and Analyzing Compound Characters*, *Ba* and *Fa* are in *Jiyun*), and means "box of recycled arrows"; 箙 is the apparatus for recovering arrows and ropes after hunting.

Let's comment on the merits and demerits of Wang and Liu.

The phrase "*bo* was mounted in semicircular machinery" is not clearly expressed. 箙 is the so-called semicircular machine (*Selections from the Sichuan Han Portrait Bricks in the Chongqing Museum*, Liu and Shen Congwen all used this saying), which is a kind of "bamboo and wood frame" (Shen's words), can be inserted into the ground when fixed, and can be pulled out to carry when walking. Four shafts, like spinning spindles, are installed inside the frame, which can be turned to wind the rope. This winding shaft was found in No. 5 Hanjiang Huchang Western Han tomb in Jiangsu Province and can be regarded as an upgraded version of *bo*. Wang's opinion is incorrect.

籤 is the shade of the tree on the bank of the pool, which is far-fetched. The picture of the tree has fallen out of leaves, and the two shooters have no shade. And the word 籤 is a bamboo head, which should be a bamboo product made by hand. The *Book of Rites* recorded: "During the breeding and mating season, indiscriminate hunting is prohibited, and all kinds of hunting tools and veterinary drugs are strictly controlled out of the city gates." Chen Hao noted: "There are seven types of hunting equipment that cannot be taken out of the city because it is against morality." 籤 belongs to seven types of hunting equipment. The environment in the picture is located in the countryside beyond the nine gates, so there is no need to set up 籤 at all.

The third paragraph of Wang's text is taken from Sun Ji's *Material Culture of the Han Dynasty*: "The rice in neat rows is pinched by two men and one woman with a sickle. The two men before them mowed the stalks with a skull for composting.

In the past, it was thought that *ba* was also used for harvesting grain. The image on this brick disproves this theory." (The gender of the characters and the "composting" are conjectures.) However, this again seems to contradict the statement of the *Six Secret Teachings · Agricultural Tools*. Perhaps. Therefore, Liu avoided the words "rice stalks," "rice stalks," and "grass stalks," and chose the Sichuan word "cereal grass" instead. *Yigou*, in Liu's text, is a kind of large sickle. It is a tool for mowing grain and grass. (It is called *Zhao* or *Guo* in Jiang, Huai, Chen, and Chu. It is also called *Gou*, *Lian*, and *Qie* in the area west of Hagu Pass.) It may coexist with the word "铗" to be examined.

The season in the portrait is "the harvest season of autumn" in Liu's text. It can be further defined as the third month of the autumn season. According to the *Book of Rites*, the month's events include "the coming of the wild geese" and "the yellowing of the grass and trees." The related human activities include "the preparation of agriculture for harvest" and "coil the horse and bend the bow, take the arrow and go hunting" (and then "sacrificing birds in all directions"). The portraits correspond to these.

According to the *Study of Ancient Chinese Costumes* by Shen Congwen, the hairstyles of the eight people in the portraits are all "cone bun"; as for the costumes, the six people in charge of farming all wear "short clothes with waist." Shen also said, "The role of the arrow is not straight in the arrow, but the arrow wrapped around the long neck of the wild goose." The winding arrow statement is with a vector to pay to wind the neck of the geese. This situation has been seen in the shooting pattern of the silver-inlaid bronze pot of the Warring States period in Baihuatan, Chengdu, and other records like "add ribbons to tighten the neck of the geese" in *Xinxu*, the documents of the Western Han Dynasty documents. However, it is not shown on this brick or is deliberately omitted.

In summary, we have made this analysis.

The brick is divided into two, independent of each other and as one, with the feeling of a split screen for film and television. These portraits are the visual illustration and artistic expression of the following records.

> "The land of Shu Prefecture is fertile with ample river water, fertile fields, dense mountains and forests, bamboo and wood, vegetables, food, and fruits in abundance ... The people eat rice and fish and forget about the worries of disaster years."
>
> —*Book of Han · Treatise on Geography*

> "Weeding with a scythe, shooting down geese and ducks with a bow and arrow."
>
> —WANG BAO, *Boy's Testament*

> "Shoot short arrows, wrap ribbons around them, shoot down white geese, and drive them."
>
> —SIMA XIANGRU, *Zixu Fu*

The upper part is the "Shooting Geese": in the autumn month, the grass and trees are yellow and fallen; on the outskirts of the river, there are two people (perhaps they are both military officials of the Han Dynasty) dressed in military attire (the style seems to be like that of the warriors in the Jinqueshan Han tomb in Linyi, Shandong), opening their bows to shoot geese (but no arrow or that has been shot, maybe for the sake of the picture and deliberately left white), the arrow (left perforated) tied to a long thin rope tied to the 檄 on the ground; the second half is the "harvest picture": Three peasants in cone buns and short suits, bending over, are in the field, holding a sickle to pinch off the ears of rice. On the far left is a rice delivery man, carrying a bundle of rice on his shoulders and a hand-held tool as if preparing to return.

The two images are combined to show that it is the time of another year's harvest, with flying geese in the sky, floating eiders in the water, carp playing with lotuses, and fragrant rice fields, a vivid scene of the Land of Abundance. One cannot help but think of the chanting in the *Classic of Poetry*.

> The geese are flying in the sky with their beautiful feathers.
> Let's take out short arrows and shoot geese.
> We obtained rice in October, so we can use this to make spring wine.
> I will drink with you, dear one, and grow old with you.

However, if the word "rice" is replaced by "silk reeling," the mood created in the poems of Tang and Song might be even more apt.

> The wild yard lists a few spring rocks.
> The thorny casement backs the beautiful village.
> In the early winter, I was in my leisure time farming.
> I shot down a flock of geese and cooked a fish.

> The soup is fresh because of the new geese.
> The jacket is lightly warmed by silk reeling.
> The farming family is happy at the end of the year.
> These officials may not know this kind of joy.

Addendum

After completing the above article, I saw Xu Wuwen's inscription on the rubbing copy of "Shooting and Harvest Brick," which was converted from traditional characters to simplified ones and punctuated as follows: "This is one of the Han painted bricks excavated in the suburbs of Chengdu. At the bottom of the picture is a scene of harvesting in a field: two people on the right are wielding scythes to mow the harvest, three people at the back are bending down and opening their arms to collect the harvest, and one person at the left end is carrying the crop on his left shoulder and carrying scandens with his right hand. The *Classic of Poetry · Binfeng · July* records the following sentences.

Peeling dates in August,
Harvesting Rice in October.

Take my wife and children with me,
Go together to harvest the crops in the field.

This picture depicts precisely this scene.

Above is a lotus pond with fish and eiders far away. The two people in the pond's shade are striving to open their bows and shoot the geese in the air, and the geese are frightened to fly. This brick picture depicts ancient rural production work, vivid, subtle, poetic, picturesque, complete, and adequate. In the past few decades, a maximum of a hundred Han painting bricks have been found in western Sichuan, but this brick must be the first. *Ke*, originally meaning wine vessel, probably refers to the food box. Xu's article and mine coincide and relate to the verse *July*.

Then I found an article by Wang Bingshuang, "An Analysis of Artisans in Art – Taking the Han Dynasty Portrait Brick as an Example," in which he said, "The Han Dynasty Portrait Brick is a kind of square portrait brick, which can be found in the following places: The Brick and Stone Chambers, No. 1, 2 and 10 tombs in Yangzi Mountain. The tomb in Zhaojue Temple. No. 2 tomb in Zengjiabao, and Ximenwai tomb in Chengdu, etc. In addition, about ten bricks have been excavated in the Sichuan plain and nearby areas. These bricks are the same size, 40–43 cm in height and 46–49 cm in width. From the excavation and distribution of the bricks, it can be assumed that they were all molded, so that bricks made from the same mold would appear in different tombs and locations." The one excavated in the Chengdu Plain and nearby areas should include the one excavated in 1972 in Anren Township, Dayi County, in the Sichuan Museum collection (The images are already blotchy and indecipherable).

———— ◆◆ ————

CHAPTER 19

What Could Sima Qian See of the Shu Region?

B efore he became an eminent historian, the young Sima Qian was already an
uncompromising traveler.

"Read ten-thousand books and travel ten-thousand miles" is a lifelong pursuit
for most people. Still, Sima Qian had completed it before he accepted his father's
bequest at twenty-six to begin preparations for writing the *Records of the Grand
Historian*. In the Preface to the *Records of the Grand Historian*, he has this brief
and richly written autobiography:

> I studied ancient literature when I was ten years old and traveled south
> at twenty, first to the area of Jianghuai and then to Mount Kuaiji to visit
> the cave of Yu the Great. Then I went south to Jiuyi Mountain and took a
> boat to see the Yuan and Xiang rivers. Then I went north to cross Wen and
> Si rivers, studied Confucianism in Linzi and Qufu, the old capital of Qi
> and Lu, and enjoyed the legacy of Confucius. I also attended the township
> archery in Zou County and Yishan; later, I suffered some hardships when
> passing through Po, Xue, and Pengcheng counties and finally returned
> home through Liang and Chu. Soon after, I entered the capital as an official
> and was later ordered to go on a mission to the south of Ba and Shu, visiting

Qiongdu, Zuodu, and Kunming. After the mission ended, I returned to the capital to resume my duties.

This journey, which started at the age of a young man and covered the southeast and central plains, Mr. Li Changzhi's book *The Personality and Style of Sima Qian*, has been described in Chapter 4, Section 2, so I will not repeat it here. We will only talk about the details of Sima Qian's trip to the southwest after he took up the official post, especially his western expedition to Ba Shu.

In Shu, Sima Qian saw the Wen Mountain (Mount Min) and the thousand miles of "fertile land" under the Wen Mountain, which is the Chengdu Plain today. Later, he recalled.

Bashu also has a vast fertile land, while an abundance of goblets, ginger, cinnabar, stone, copper, iron, bamboo, and wood-made appliances. In the south of Bashu, it is the Bo Road of Dian-Yue Kingdom. Bo people were taken captive to sell. Bashu is also connected to Qiongdu and Zuodu in the west, so people are selling Zuo horses and yaks from Qiongdu and Zuodu to Bashu. However, there are mountains on all sides of Bashu. There are thousands of miles of trestle roads in the mountains, which are accessible in all directions. Only the Baoxie Road controls the exit of Bashu to the north, through which the people of Bashu exchange the surplus for the needed goods.[1]

Like many ancient people, Sima Qian also entered Shu from the Baoxie Road.

At that time, "Shu berry" was already exported to the South Yue Kingdom (the capital was in present-day Guangzhou), "Shu cloth and crippled bamboo stick"[2] were shipped to the Daxia Kingdom (an ancient state in Central Asia, located in northern Afghanistan). *Dunchi* was famous in the State of Zhao, one of the Seven Warring States. *Dunchi* is a kind of taro; it's large and peerless, like a squatting owl.[3] Sima Qian probably also had seen it.

Since Shu cloth can be exported to generate foreign exchange, it proves that it is close to saturation in the Chengdu market. How about its price at that time? On the bamboo slips of the Han Dynasty found in the Juyan region of northwest

---

1. Sima Qian, *Records of the Grand Historian · Biographies of Goods and Services*, Western Han Dynasty.

2. Sima Qian, *Records of the Grand Historian · Biography of the Southwest Barbarians*, Western Han Dynasty.

3. Sima Qian, *Records of the Grand Historian · Biography of the Goods and Services*, Western Han Dynasty.

China, it is written, "Eight *zong* nineteen *pi* of Guanghan cloth, 8.5 *cun*, the value is 4,320 *qian*." Each *pi* was worth more than 227*qian*. *Zong* 稯 can also be written as 總 or 緵.

During the Han Dynasty, there were seven, eight, nine, and ten *zong* according to the specifications of the weaving, like the modern term of how many counts of yarn were used in weaving, which reflected the difference in cost and quality. In the Western Han Dynasty, during the reign of Empress *Lü*, the government provided clothing for "all the officials and staffs in the inner counties," and "the cloth was made with eight and seven *zong*."[4] During the reign of Emperor Jing, the government continued to "make the staffs wear seven *zong* cloth."[5] Seven *zong* cloth can also be called seven liters cloth. Eight strands of cloth are one *zong* or one liter. So, seven liters of cloth used 560 strands.[6] The width of the cloth is two *chi* and two *cun*, so if the cloth is ten *zong*, it means that there are 800 strands on a width of two *chi* and two *cun*.

The level of craftsmanship is so meticulous and advanced. Guanghan was established as a prefecture at the beginning of the Han Dynasty, with Guanghan County under its jurisdiction. Sanxingdui is in Guanghan, which was once a handicraft production base relied on by the imperial court. "Guanghan mainly produces gold and silverware." "The major production is lacquerware items." These statements reflect that the industrial goal of the "Gongguan" (the office that managed the government handicraft industry) in Guanghan County during the Han Dynasty seems to have been mainly to meet the needs of the upper class for household utensils. The "eight *zong* cloths of Guanghan" in the Hexi text tells us that the textile products of Sichuan had already formed a profitable local brand and could benefit the public.

The most noteworthy thing is that Sima Qian was the first celebrity in history to travel, examine, record, and promote the Dujiangyan. He wrote at a high level in *The Book of Rivers and Drains*.

"Since Yu the Great controlled the water, people diverted the southeast flow of Yellow River water from near Xingyang and built Honggou, which flowed through Song, Zheng, Chen, Cai, Cao, and Wei, and communicated the four

---

4. *Laws and Orders of the Second Year · Laws on Gold and Cloth*, the bamboo slip of the Han Dynasty, unearthed in Zhangjiashan.

5. Sima Qian, *Records of the Grand Historian · Biography of Emperor Jing*, Western Han Dynasty.

6. Zhang Shoujie, *The Proper Explanation of the Records of the Grand Historian*, Tang Dynasty.

rivers of Ji, Ru, Huai, and Si. In Chu, there were channels linking Hanshui and Yunmengze in the west, and Hangou Ditch was dug in the east to communicate with the Yangtze River and Huai River. In Wu, channels were dug to connect the three rivers and five lakes. In Qi, there were channels connecting Zi and Ji Rivers. In Shu, Li Bing, the Governor of Shu Prefecture, dug the Lidui to eliminate the flooding of froth water and explored the PI and Jian rivers to reach Chengdu directly. These waterways are navigable, and the excess water is used for irrigation. The people enjoy the benefits brought by the channels. These main channels flow through the place and often cut many small ditches for irrigating the fields, tens of thousands; it is unnecessary to elaborate."

Shu Shou Bing (蜀守冰) is the official name of Li Bing of the Qin State in the Warring States. Lidui (离碓) was referred to as the Dujiangyan; it could avoid floods, navigation, and irrigate the fields. At the end of *The Book of Rivers and Drains*, Sima Qian recalled: "I traveled south to climb Mount Lu and saw the Jiujiang River dredged by Yu the Great, southeast to Kuaiji, climbed Mount Gusu, and looked at the five lakes from Mount Gusu; east to examine the Luorui, Dapi, Yinghe, and toured the channels that diverted the waters of Huai, Si, Ji, Luo, and Luo; west to see the water conservancy projects of Minshan and Lidui in Shu; and north from Longmen up to Shuofang. I was deeply impressed: the benefits of water to humanity or the harm caused are too great!"

This time, he will be more accurate in the positioning of Dujiangyan: the west of China → Shu → under Mount Min → Li Dui. It seems that the meaning of "Bing chiseling Lidui" and "Yu dredging the nine rivers" are comparable, which accidentally opened the door for later people to praise Li Bing for his "merit after God Yu" or the precedent of "the work like God Yu."

To give thanks to Sima Qian, the ancestors of Dujiangyan built Taishigong Temple and Xizhan Hall next to the weir. These places do not exist today but are recorded in history and can be passed on for a long time.

———— •✦• ————

CHAPTER 20

Chengdu in the Words of Zeng Jian, Translator of Tsangyang Gyatso's Love Poems

In 1982, the Tibetan People's Publishing House published *A Study of Tsangyang Gyatso and His Love Songs (Compilation of Materials)*, including English and Chinese translations by Yu Daoquan, Liu Jiaju, Zeng Jian, Zhuang Jing, and others. Perhaps the book did not attract enough response because of the small print run.

In 2010, the lyrics of the closing song of the famous movie: *Do Not Disturb, Part Two* included the following lines:

> Since we knew each other when we saw each other,
> how could we have seen each other without seeing each other?
> If we didn't know each other, would we still see each other the same?
> I can't say goodbye to you.
> Thus, I won't have to live and die thinking about you.

If listeners are careful, they will discover this is a Tibetan love song by the renowned poet and monk, the Sixth Dalai Lama, Tsangyang Gyatso (1683– 1706?), translated into Chinese by Zeng Jian (1892–1968) as a seven-line stanza.

The only difference is that the last line of Zeng's original text is written as "to avoid missing you so much."[1]

It was this short translation of the poem that brought Zeng Jian back to readers' attention after decades of silence, and professional scholarly papers such as *The World Can Be Perfect: An Exploration of Zeng Jian's Translation of the Sixth Dalai Lama's Sixty · Six Love Songs* were published one after another.

So, who was Zeng Jian?

According to the Preface of *Kang Xing Ji*, published by Bashu Press in June 2021 (written by Zeng Jian, collated by Cun Tie Sun, in three volumes), Zeng Jian was a native of Xuyong, Sichuan. His style name was 圣言 (*Shengyan*, which means oracle). And he has another name, *Shenyan* (慎言), which means cautious in speech. He was later known as *Cuntie Laoren* (寸铁老人), which means an older man with little iron. *Miaoweng* (眇翁) was his nickname as well. It means a blind, more aged man.

In 1912, he was admitted to Peking University, where he studied under the master of Chinese studies Huang Kan, known as "Deputy Dean of Huang School." During his studies, he was also the chief writer of the *Republican Daily* in Beijing. He graduated in 1917 with a bachelor's degree in Chinese literature. Subsequently, he entered the military and political circles to earn a living. He served as secretary of Liu Yujiu's division, secretary of Li Jiayu, secretary of Tian Songyao, secretary of Liu Wenhui, and magistrate of Lezhi, Shifang, Jiangbei, and Ya'an counties in Sichuan Province. He was the academic dean of the Sichuan College of Studies of Ancient Chinese Civilization, a member of the Sichuan Senate, the Mongolian-Tibetan Committee of the Republic of China, and secretary general of the Provisional Senate of Xikang Province.

In his bones, Zeng Jian was always a scholar, during which he wrote many poems and songs in newspapers and magazines. In 1947, he resigned from his post as magistrate of Ya'an County. He was appointed professor of the Chinese Department at Sichuan University and served as head of the department and director of the Institute of Liberal Arts.

The poems and writings of Zeng Jian include many chapters describing Chengdu's scenery, sights, and folklore. And with the publication of his

---

1. In Zeng's translation of "Sixty-six Love Songs of the Sixth Dalai Lama (see Fig. 12)" in *Kangdao Monthly*, vol. 1, no. 8, 1939, and in the manuscript in the family collection of his granddaughter Zeng Qian (see Fig. 13), both are written as "to avoid I miss you so hard."

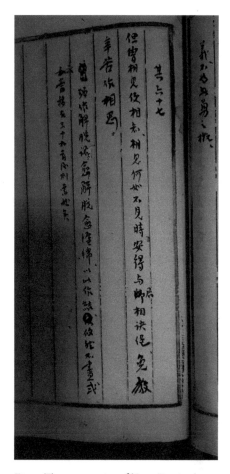

Fig. 12 Zeng Jian's translation of "Sixty-six Love Songs of the Sixth Dalai Lama" in *Kangdao Monthly*, vol. 1, no. 8, 1939.

Fig. 13 The manuscript of Zeng Jian in the collection of Ms. Zeng Qian.

posthumous book, *Kang Xing Ji*, it is time to include it in the study of Tianfu culture.

Chengdu: A Plain City with a View of Snow-Capped Mountains

Chengdu has been honored with many titles since ancient times, and in recent years it has been named the "Park City under the Snowy Mountains." Seventy sightings of snowy mountains were reported in Chengdu in 2020, up from 65 in 2019, 56 in 2018, and 50 in 2017, a record high in recent years. Among them, the peak season for mountain viewing in Chengdu is July, August, and September. On August 24, 2020, a photographer in Jintang, Chengdu, set a record for taking a photo of Mount Gongga from 282 kilometers away. For four years in a row, mountain viewing has been recorded on all 30 days of July except for July 31. Therefore, July deserves to be the lucky month for mountain viewing in Chengdu.

Back in July 1954, Zeng Jian also saw the snow-capped mountains from Chengdu. After "having a good time," he wrote a song called *Song for the Western Mountains after the Rain*. There is a small preface in the song.

"Western Mountain, and Wenling snow peaks, across the state and county hundreds of miles, can be seen from the Chengdu plain. The treacherous peaks are a wonder of the world. However, it is often in the clouds and fog, not too clear, and not visible until the Qingming Festival. The time that can be seen is also for a short time. What Chengdu people can see is also a hazy view. The heavy rain cleared in the early autumn of the Jiawu Year, and the waning sun was still bright. This mountain suddenly emerged in front of us ..."

In the opinion of Lu You, a poet of the Song Dynasty, Chengdu has "two no's." The first is Chengdu has no mountains, and the second is no lychees. Zhou Xun of the Qing Dynasty also said that flat lands surround Chengdu, and the nearest mountain to Chengdu is 30 to 35 kilometers away. There are older people in the city who don't travel much, and they don't know what shape the mountains are. This is an exaggeration regarding the urban area of Chengdu. Du Fu, a poet of the Tang Dynasty whose eyes were relatively more open, wrote a poem:

> The window holds the western peak's snow of a thousand autumns,
> my gate moors for eastern Wu, a ten-thousand league boat.

Du Mu, another poet of the Tang Dynasty, also wrote:

> The city connects the western peak's snow,
> the sails of ten-thousand miles link the bridge.

The western peak is the Western Mountains, which is said to be based in Chengdu, and sometimes you can see the mountains in the west hundreds of miles away, as long as the atmospheric visibility is good enough.

From Zeng Jian's account, although the population of Chengdu in the 1950s was in the millions, the passion and hobby of mountain watching had not yet been developed. One is because it's too rare that "see the mountains for only a few days a year." The other is because citizens are busy with their daily lives and have no leisure time. So, Zeng Jian reminisced about Du Fu's leisurely years in Chengdu:

> The beauty of the peaks stands unabated,
> Du Fu's poems are rightfully renowned.
> Five Great Mountains' beauty forever sounds.
> The western peak's snow is a wonder to behold.

It's a pity that this poetic advertisement of the entire Mount Min by Du Fu has now been artificially narrowed down to the endorsement of a mountain peak (The Western Snow Peak).

Dunchi 蹲鸱²: A Magical Product on a Fertile Field

Perhaps as a deliberate tribute to the poet-saint Du Fu, Zeng Jian also has three five-word ancient poems directly titled "West Mountain."

The first poem is about Qingcheng Mountain, and the first line is the pet phrase of the people in Dujiangyan today: "Four hundred kilometers of Qingcheng." Of course, in the Republican era, the locals were proud of this, such as the couplet made by Chen Yaosheng, the director of the Bureau of Tax in Guan County: "Four hundred kilometers of Qingcheng's fertile fields, all of which came from the Governor." The Governor is Li Bing.

The second poem is about the Min River and Mount Min:

> The snow melted, and the river rose.
> The auspicious clouds rise from Shu Mountain.
> Jingluo is a symbol of good luck.
> The people get a great harvest of dunchi every year.
> When will we see this beautiful sight?
> I hold my cheek and wait for the autumn wind.

---

2. 蹲鸱 Dunchi is a native product of the Chengdu plain. It's a big taro, and its shape resembles a crouching owl. This is documented in the *Records of the Grand Historian · Biographies of Merchants*, which proves that it has been cultivated in the Chengdu plain for thousands of years.

And at the bottom of the line, he said, "This mountain is easy to see in autumn." The poem echoes the content and mood of *Song for the Western Mountains after the Rain*. The poem has three allusions, which should be interpreted a little.

The first is the dazzling 井络 *Jingluo*. The astrologers, in order to use celestial changes to divine the fortune of the earth, will be the heavenly stars and earthly areas correspondence, unified, and put forward the concept of 分野 *Fenye*. East Jing is the first mansion to the south of The Twenty-Eight Mansions. (i.e., 井 *Jing* mansion is east of the Yujing star. So, it's called East Jing. Now it belongs to Gemini.) The *Fenye* of East Jing includes Shu. So, the land of the Shu capital is also called 井络之野 *Jingluo Zhiye*.

Taoists also believe that the essence of mountains and rivers can rise into the universe of the column of stars. *Hetu Kuodi Xiang*, an Astro book at the end of the Western Han Dynasty, said: "Above the land of Mount Min is the star of *Jingluo*. The emperor in this place can make the country prospers, and the gods give their blessing because the essence of Mount Min rises to the Jing star in the sky."

The literati generally accepted this concept, such as Zuo Si said in *Shu Capital Rhapsody*, "Far to the essence of Mount Min, rising as the Jingluo star in the sky."

And Guo Pu wrote in *Jiang Fu*, "The essence of Mount Min is dazzling on East Jing star."

The second is the *dunchi* in the fertile field. There is this in the *Records of the Grand Historian · Biography of the Goods and Services*:

> The ancestors of the Zhuo family in Sichuan, originally from the State of Zhao, became wealthy from their iron smelting business. After Qin destroyed the State of Zhao, the Zhuo family was forced to leave. They were taken into captivity, and only a husband and wife pushed their carts toward the designated relocation site. Those who were forced to move at the same time, as long as they had some money, were scrambling to bribe the officials who led the group, asking to be placed in a slightly closer place, settling in the area of Jiameng Pass. Only Zhuo said, "This place is small and barren. I heard that under Mount Min is fertile land, and the land produces big taro, so we can feed ourselves and not die of hunger."

About this big taro like an owl, later there are folk songs like this:

The great famine is not hungry.

Shu has *dunchi*.

The great drought is not chaos.

Shu has Guanghan.[3]

Before the Dujiangyan, this *dunchi* may have always existed; after horizontal soil fertilization, it should have achieved a bumper crop. Otherwise, it would not be well known outside of Sichuan as well.

The third is to hold the cheek to see the mountain. This allusion is from *A New Account of the Tales of the World: Rudeness and Arrogance*.

Wang Ziyou served as a cavalry counselor under General Heng Wen. Heng said to Wang, "You have been in my mansion for a long time, and you should become prime minister." When Wang Ziyou heard this, he did not answer at first but only kept looking up high, holding his hand to his cheek and saying, "The cool air comes in the morning from the western mountains."

It is important to note that Wang Ziyou's West Mountain is not Du Fu's West Mountain. Perhaps Zeng Jian liked this allusion so much that he couldn't resist using it again at the end of the third poem: "The west comes with a lot of cool air, and now it's in the old man's poem." The poem is an excellent example of how to use the 'cool air' allusion to the 'Western Mountains.'

Wang Xizhi: A Lifelong Longing for Tianfu

The third poem in Zeng Jian's "The Western Mountains" again refers to Du Fu:

The window faces a thousand peaks of snow.

A good story that captures the beauty in this peak of snow.

Millions of guests can meet Du Fu.

And I saw Wang Xizhi.

The sages have left,

but the beauty remains here to imbue.

---

3. These four lines can be seen on the ancient monument and noted in the *Guanzhi Wenzheng*, Volume 14, during the era of the Republic of China.

The first and third lines are obviously the application of "The window holds the western peak's snow of a thousand autumns." It's clear, and no need to explain more. As for the relationship between Wang Xizhi and the west mountain, it is a legend worth revisiting.

Wang Xizhi, like Zuo Si, had never been to Sichuan in his life, but this did not prevent them from sending their love to Sichuan, which was more sincere and passionate than Song Lian ever had. He Yudu, a Kui Prefecture official who was in the same period as Song Lian, wrote the following words at the beginning of his book, *Yibu Tanzi*.

In his life, Wang Xizhi loved the landscape of Sichuan most, and he was eager to visit Sichuan. But this elegant wish was never realized. Thousands of years later, his calligraphic works can still compete with the beauty of Sichuan's landscapes.

Wang Xizhi, also named Wang Yishao, was a native of Linyi, Langya (now Linyi, Shandong), who later moved to Shanyin, Kuaiji (now Shaoxing, Zhejiang), and in his later years lived in seclusion in Shan County (now Yingzhou, Zhejiang). He had a lifelong fascination with Sichuan. He wrote to his friends in different areas at different times. He could not help overflowing with words, either saying, "If I am ordered to Guanlong and Bashu, I will not resist," or suspecting that Yang Xiong and Zuo Si's "Shu Capital Rhapsody" were not complete enough, and planning "It is indeed a monumental event to climb Mount Wenling and hover in Mount Emei. Whenever I think of it, my heart has already flown there." Even in his twilight years, he was still undeterred. He promised his old friend Zhou Fu, the governor of Yizhou: "I hope to visit Sichuan and see Mount Min with my own eyes. This is not me nagging repeatedly; you must take care of your health and wait for my arrival. My words are not empty words; if this destiny exists, it will be a good story." Zeng Jian's poem within "A good story" is from this literary quotation.

According to He Yudu's explanation, "纹领 *Wenling* is the ancient writing of 岷岭 *Minling*." Zeng Jian wrote it in 汶岭 *Wenling*. Lǐng 领 and lǐng 岭 are different, but they have the same meaning.

Mount Min with its peaks, the fire wells and salt wells in Qiongzhou, Pengxi, and Fushun, the "summer frost and hail" in Emei Mountain, and other such "wonders of the mountains and rivers" have haunted the soul of the "Sage of Calligraphy" for this dreaming place in his whole lifetime.

Tonghua Dong: Sichuan Proverb Can Be Incorporated into Poetry

Zeng Jian has three poems entitled *Tonghua Dong*, the first of which reads:

The spring cold in the third month is heavy,
and it is called Tonghua Dong.
The Tonghua is frozen,
but not to freeze the phoenix.

What is meant by *Tonghua Dong?*

In *Huifeng Cihua* it is written, "Sichuan dialect can be directly quoted in the poems; there is one concept called 'Tonghua Dong,' which is the spring cold in April of the lunar calendar." This is what the author, Kuang Zhouyi, heard from others, which may be different from the fact. Zeng Jian has mentioned this in the preface of *Tonghua Dong*.

In the third month of the lunar calendar, the cold weather decreases in Sichuan. The tung trees bloom, so the Sichuan people named it "Tonghua Dong," which means the frozen tung blossom.

The time in this saying is correct. Decades later, I heard the same: "The poor man, the poor man, you do not boast! The tung blossoms will be frozen in the third month."

There are several versions of this Sichuan proverb; the word types are more disparate.

Cattle boys, you do not boast. There are still 24 days of tung blossoms.

The tung trees bloom just in the Qingming season. There are three kinds of weather during Qingming Festival; the first one is when the tung trees bloom. Coinciding with the beginning of the third lunar month, spring's cold is still crisp. In the old days, those who lacked clothes and clothing saw that tung trees had blossomed, thinking that the weather was finally going to heat up; they were happy and enthusiastic, forgetting that the temperature was unstable. And a little carelessness could lead to a cold. "Wear more clothes in spring, fewer clothes in autumn, and no miscellaneous diseases" is true.

As a native of Sichuan, Zeng Jian naturally knew this widely circulated Sichuan proverb and wrote it into his poem. This adds to the "poet's wonder" of "using the commonplace as elegance and the old as the new."[4]

---

4. Quoting the words of Huang Tingjian, a famous poet of the Northern Song Dynasty.

CHAPTER 21

————◆◆◆————

Joseph Needham's Visit to Dujiangyan

D
r. Joseph Needham, the famous British historian of science and author of the magnificent book *Science and Civilization in China*, is an old friend of the Chinese people and visited China nine times between the 1940s and 1980s. The last time, he was already 86 years old and went to Qingcheng Mountain on a sedan chair.

His full name was Noel Joseph Terence Montgomery Needham, and Joseph Li was his Chinese name. In late 1942, as a professor of biochemistry at Cambridge University and a member of the British Cultural and Scientific Delegation to China, Joseph Needham came to China for the first time, as he had longed to do. At that time, *Xinhua Daily* called him "Mr. Needham, the famous British biologist." He then stayed in China as a science counselor at the British Embassy in China and as the director of the Sino-British Science Cooperation Office until 1946. During this period, with close cooperation and help from his then-secretaries Huang Xingzong and Cao Tianqin, he drove a touring car allotted by the British Embassy. He converted from a dilapidated ambulance, tossing and turning all the way and running through half of China, covering Yunnan, Guizhou, Sichuan, Shaanxi, Gansu, Hunan, and Fujian provinces.

One of the essential locations was Dujiangyan, "one of the greatest projects in China." In 1943, the ancient weir, which had undergone many vicissitudes, welcomed Needham and his colleagues. In the same year, he published a series of articles entitled "Science in Western Sichuan," including a section on "Irrigation Works in Guan County," in which he recorded: "The undisguised religious worship of Yu the Great, a great water engineer, is quite significant. Not far northwest of Chengdu is a town called Guan County, where one can find one of the world's most excellent irrigation projects. The Min River, which originates on the Tibetan Plateau's edge, diverges here. A large gap was cut through the mountains. At certain seasons of the year, water was diverted into this gap using dams and diversion weirs, thus creating an artificial river that irrigates 500,000 acres of land through 1,200 kilometers of channels of various sizes. The most noteworthy aspect of this project is that it was built in about 256 BCE by Li Bing, the Governor of Shu, and has been used ever since.

Meanwhile, not content to view the project in purely practical terms, the Chinese, with their innate ability to deify mere mortals, built a magnificent temple to Li Bing on the outermost ridge of the mountain where the river flows through the mouth of the chisel. A little further down the river, on a tree-lined hill in an equally pleasant setting, they also built a temple for Li Bing's son, Li Erlang, a water engineer. Note the contrast between the front part of Li Bing's temple, where incense is abundant, and the other courtyard, where numerous models intended to improve the project are displayed. The engineers used the temple of Erlang as a dormitory, while the altar and courtyard of Yu the Great became the offices of the hydrological management committee …

Many things need to be corrected in the descriptions here. For example, Guan County is a small county, not a small town. The Min River originates in the western foothills of the Moba East Mountains in Manzhang Township, Dari County, Guoluo Tibetan Autonomous Prefecture, Qinghai Province, not in Tibet. The so-called "big gap," or "chisel mouth," is the Baopingkou or Bottle-Neck Channel. The "river flowing through the mouth of the mountain's outermost cross-ridge" refers to the Lidui. "Li Bing Temple" on the mountain is the Fulongguan. At that time, the front hall of the temple was dedicated to a statue of Li Bing (see Fig. 14), who was wearing a crown and boots, with bright eyes and sat properly, and his hand holding an imperial tablet. The statue of Erlang, Li Bing's son, was set in the back hall of the temple.[1] This is just the opposite of the Erlang Temple (i.e., Two Kings Temple), where Erlang is worshipped at the front and Li Bing at the back.

---

1. Wanyan Chongshi, "The Monument of the Reconstruction the Temple of Duke Li, Governor of Shu in Qin Dynasty, King of Fuze Xingji Tongyou, ordained by His Majesty."

Fig. 14 The statue of Li Bing at Fulongguan, which no longer exists today.

The so-called "divine altar and courtyard of Yu the Great," the King Yu Palace on Yulei Mountain.

Since Needham was a first time visitor, he needed to learn more about the situation of Dujiangyan, so such omissions are justifiable. It is interesting to note that his historicization of the legendary figure of Li Erlang as a water engineer is the opposite path of the Chinese "innate ability to deify mere mortals."

In 1958, Needham came to China for the third time, the second time to Dujiangyan, and inspected and photographed the Bridge Anlan, which he called the "Guan County Bridge." Later, in his book *Science and Civilization in China*, he wrote: "The most notable successor to Yu the Great was the construction of the Dujiangyan, a great irrigation project, in the third century BCE, by Li Bing of the Qin Dynasty in Guan County, northwest of Chengdu, Sichuan Province, which became famous throughout the world. The project, built by Li Bing and completed by his son (Li Erlang), was a 735-mile-long diversion canal in the Min River to irrigate 500,000 acres of farmland. A local temple was built to worship him, and stone monuments were put down to record his achievements." This understanding is almost the same as in 1943, except that the length of the aqueduct, "1200 kilometers," was changed to 735 miles. "The stone monuments were put down to record his achievements" refers to the stone inscriptions in the Two Kings Temple, such as "Pour the beach deep and make a weir low."

The same book also says: "The date of the original construction of the bridge is not known, but given the folkloric nature of the general principle, and the talents of Li Bing and his contemporaries, there seems little reason why the bridge should not date back to that period. It must have been before the Song Dynasty." Sadly, he is also incorrect in this inference. Li Bing built more than one bridge, but they were all in the urban area of Chengdu (see *Chronicles of Huayang* for details) and not over the Min River. Bridge Anlan was built, coincidentally in the Song Dynasty; the specific year, the first year of the Chunhua reign in the Northern Song Dynasty (Wei liaoweng, *Yongkangjun Pingshiqiao Mianfuyi Ji*).

As an international friend, it was rare for Needham to visit Dujiangyan several times to praise its greatness and to promote it to the Western world. These shortcomings in his writings are the starting point for a new generation of scholars, and sometimes it is okay to be too critical or not to be critical when we think about it. As Mr. Qian Mu sagely teaches, we should have "warmth and respect" for history.

CHAPTER 22

———◆◆◆———

The Past Life of the Qingyang Palace

Qingyang Palace is a Taoist temple in Chengdu's second section of the first ring road. When it comes to its origin, many people will mention the legend: Laozi wrote the *Taoist Scriptures* for Guanling Yinxi. And he told Yinxi, 'After a thousand days of your monastic life, find me at the Qingyang Si in Chengdu.' The Qingyang Si is today's Qingyang Palace. Another version is what Laozi wrote for Yinxi is the *Tao Te Ching*. The original source of this story is the *Shu Ben Ji*, also known as the *Biographies of the Kings of Shu*.

Speculation One: Qingyang Palace Is a Taoist Temple in the Shu Han Kingdom

First, the question arises: who is the author of the *Shu Ben Ji*? *Imperial Reader of the Taiping Era* and *Universal Geography of the Taiping Era* needs to be indicated. And the *Chronicles of Huayang* records: "Sima Xiangru, Yan Junping, Yang Ziyun, Yang Cheng Zixuan, Zheng Boyi, Yin Pengcheng, Qiao Changshi, Ren Jishi, and others collected the biographies of each episode to form this *Chronicles of Huayang*." Sima Xiangru, Yan Zun, Yang Xiong, Yang Cheng Zixuan, Zheng Jin, Yin Gong, Qiao Zhou, and Ren Xi all wrote the *Shu Ben Ji*. But except for Yang and Qiao, which are quoted, the rest of the *Benji* is not credible.

So, is the section "The Qingyang Si is today's Qingyang Palace" from Yang Xiong or Qiao Zhou? With some general knowledge of Taoism, one would know that the latter is more likely. At the end of the Eastern Han Dynasty, Zhang Ling entered Shu and created Tianshi Taoism, and the beginnings of Taoism matured. Yang Xiong was born in the Western Han Dynasty, and there were no Taoist buildings like Qingyang Palace in Chengdu. But Qiao Zhou was a minister of Shu Han in the Three Kingdoms. Chen Shou, the author of the famous historical work *Records of the Three Kingdoms*, was under his tutelage. The first person to quote Qiao Zhou's *Shu Ben Ji* was Pei Songzhi, the commentator of *Records of the Three Kingdoms*. Taoism was still emerging, and it was not impossible to have a "Qingyang Palace" standing in the capital city of Shu Han.

Speculation Two: Qingyang Si Is the Market of Chengdu

Compared to Qingyang Palace, the more likely existence of the Shu Han Dynasty is the Qingyang Si.

The southern part of Chengdu was originally a commercial area and later expanded to the south of the Pi River (Neijiang) outside the city. Hence, the name of the city gate is "Market Bridge Gate," and the bridge is called "Market Bridge." A market is a place of buying and selling. Because two rivers flow here, there is enough transportation, and it was initially Chengdu's transportation hub and goods distribution place. Since Emperor Wu of the Han Dynasty adopted Tang Meng, Sima Xiangru's proposal to open up the southwest and chisel road to transport food, the business became more and more prosperous, the population increased, and thus gradually to the city outside the southwest between the two rivers developed into "south market." It is located across the river from Cheguan City and Jinguan City on both sides of the Jian River.

The South Market area was south of the Market Bridge, the area around the present-day Xijiaochang, and included the Qingyang Si, where black sheep were traded. Qing is also known as black. The name of Qingyang Main Street in Qingyang District was originally named "Qingyang Si Street," which should also be named after the Qingyang Si.

Xuanzhong Guan: The Real Predecessor of the Qingyang Palace

During the Tang Dynasty, the royal family attached great importance to Taoism, believing that Laozi was Li Er and posthumously honoring him as the founder of the Li clan and "Emperor Xuan Yuan." In this way, the royal family elevated its cultural lineage. In addition, Emperor Xuanzong of Tang also personally annotated the *Tao Te Ching* and made the scholars study it. In the twenty-ninth year of the Kaiyuan Reign (741), he also ordered the two capitals (Chang'an and Luoyang) and the prefectures to set up temples of Emperor Xuan Yuan. The capital temple was called "Xuan Yuan Palace," and the prefecture's temple was called "Ziji Palace."

In Chengdu, there was no need to establish the Ziji Palace because there was already a Taoist temple. Before Emperor Xizong entered Shu, there was a "Xuanzhong Guan," located in the Qingyang Si in Chengdu, where the statue of Laozi was enshrined in the main hall. After Xizong followed Xuanzong's footsteps and arrived in Chengdu, he changed the name of "Xuanzhong Guan" to "Qingyang Palace" by decree based on *Shu Ben Ji*, perhaps to avoid the taboo of Xuanzong.

Records of Reverence for Taoism Through the Ages by Du Guangting contains: Emperor Xizong of Tang fled to Sichuan, and on the night of August 29, in the second year of the Zhonghe Reign (882), he ordered the royal clansman Li Teli and the Taoist priest Li Wuwei to set up an altar at Xuanzhong Guan, the "old place of the birth of Hunyuan," to pray for peace. Suddenly, they saw a rainbow light as big as a bullet, gradually becoming bright. They ran out of the hall and into the bamboo forest in the southeast, jumping and skipping to the southwest corner under the plum tree and disappearing. The people concerned immediately, depression here three feet, dug up a brick. The brick was engraved with floral patterns and seal characters, and the engraving was so clean that it did not look artificial. When carefully identified, the seal characters could make up a prophetic phrase: "Tai Shang Ping Zhong He Zai." The words "Huanyuan" and "Tai Shang" refer to Laozi, while "Zhong He Zai" refers to Huang Chao's rebellion.

On the first day of the ninth month, Chen Jingxuan, the Privy Counselor of the Xichuan Military Governor, reported to Emperor Xizhong.

"The great benevolence of His Majesty the Emperor spreads throughout the country, and the supreme morality rises to the heavenly realm. So, various talismans and prophecies became increasingly frequent, and auspicious signs appeared. The Supreme Lord had already passed down an order to remove the scourge of Huang Chao's rebellious party completely. This order was given in explicit language, written in ancient seal script. This was enough to show that the demon invaders' *qi* was extinguished and that the emperor must live forever. Knowing the date of recovering the capital would also be the arrival of the day of peace in the world."

Emperor Xizong was so happy that he bestowed gifts on Li Teli, Li Wuwei, and Chen Jingxuan and issued an edict on the 21st.

"Tai Shang Xuan Yuan Emperor and his disciple Mr. Wen Shi told the true scriptures on the platform and agreed to meet later at the Qingyang Si; they took the cloud ride and flew to the sky. According to the legend of the Immortal Records, the earth's iconography contains that since King Zhao of the Zhou Dynasty to today, there have been more than 2,000 years of silent scenery, and the foundation has been firmly established. Now, because of the emperor's presence, the spirit bestowed by the emperor is obvious, and the special light jumps in front of the court, and the spirit seal is affirmed under the tree. The brick contains ancient colors, and the wording is verified to show that the disaster of Zhonghe wants to be pacified. The auspicious symbol of the thick earth is present, sufficient to show the blessing of the Xuanqiong and the auspiciousness of the Holy Ancestor, which will annihilate the warriors and the cause of Zhongxing. It is necessary to pass on the book of brief and show the world. The official has been sent to the historian, ready to order the record compilation and still mold the text, notice of all provinces and military units. The temple can be renamed 'Qingyang Palace' and build halls and buildings. In recent years, about two hectares, the fields next to the temple distributed more planted onions and garlic to the people. The sacred place of Taoism is not good with this smell fumigation. The emperor has given money 200 Guan, ordered to take back these lands, still managed by the government, the income from the fields, forever belong to the Taoist temple."

On October 7, the emperor ordered the civil engineering works for the construction of the Qingyang Palace to be supervised by the official Guo Zuntai. The funds for the building came from the emperor's internal treasury appropriation.

Since the acquisition of auspiciousness to the month of Kuichou, the bandits near Chengdu, one after another, were captured and killed. Within a few months, Sichuan restored the years of peace. Emperor Xizong inspected the Qingyang Palace, issued rewards to the people concerned, and again issued an edict: "Tai Shang Laojun rewarded bright rays, which appeared in the Qingyang Palace. According to the ritual should be extraordinarily revered, and all the materials used in the construction of Qingyang Palace must be the best. The Ziji Palace of each province, state, and prefecture in the country should appoint capable officials to follow the rules and regulations of the Qingyang Palace to decorate and send highly skilled Taoist priests to pay respects." Qingyang Palace model has become the model of the Ziji Palace around the country.

It was the month of Yimao, reported the recovery of the capital, and the prophecy of the "Ping Zhonghe Zai" was finally fulfilled.

In year 4 of the Zhonghe Reign (884), Emperor Xizong of Tang issued an edict to the Hanlin Bachelor and Minister of Defense, Yue Penggui, to write the *Inscription of the Qingyang Palace in Xichuan* and promulgated it to the whole empire.

"To indicate that the royal family is the descendant of the gods and is blessed by the spirit of Tai Shang Lao Jun in heaven for a thousand generations and a long time." The inscription reads, "Qingyang Si, according to the *Shu Ben Ji*, was the second birthplace of the Great Emperor Tai Shang Xuan Yuan. So Tai Shang Lao Jun took the green child of Qing Di, transformed into a sheep, and came to Shu, riding on a purple cloud to the Ziji Palace and descending auspiciousness to the palace." The transformation into a sheep is a literary imagination, but later generations believed it. He Geng, the Tongpan of Chengdu Prefecture in the Southern Song Dynasty, wrote his note in the poem *The Qingyang Palace*: "According to Zhao Yuedao's *Records of Chengdu*, the Qingyang Palace is where Laozi descended to earth on a green sheep, and there are still platforms preserved."

Based on the Tang text, Xie Shouhao, a Taoist priest of the Southern Song Dynasty, wrote *The Holy Writ of Hunyuan*, which makes the connection between Laozi and Chengdu more specific and suspenseful: In the 25th year of King Zhao of the Zhou Dynasty (491 BCE), Laozi was born to the family of Li Taiguan in the State of Shu. In the 27th year of King Zhao, Laozi met Yinxi at Qingyang Si. His goatee was removed, and he became immortal and went away.

The auspicious, split, I'm afraid, all the literary fabrications. The only reliable thing is the fact that Qingyang Palace was built in the Tang Dynasty. Therefore, Fu Chongju of the late Qing Dynasty wrote it as "Ancient Temple of the Tang Dynasty" in the *General Overview of Chengdu*, which is exceptionally correct.

Bronze Sheep in Ming and Qing Dynasties

To make the "green sheep" come to life, a bronze sheep was cast into the palace in the Ming Dynasty, which was as big as an elk. Later disappeared; some people estimated that it was lost due to "the Rebellion of Zhang Xianzhong" or was taken by Zhang Xianzhong to melt down to make money, which is not true. Since Wang Shizhen "saw it in Shu" in 1672, and only later was it "stolen by someone," the bronze sheep was stolen between 1672 and 1696, when Zhang Xianzhong's tomb was already bending and bowing.

In the first year of the Yongzheng Reign (1723), Zhang Penghe, an honest official alias Xinyangzi, bought back a single-horned bronze sheep from Beijing and moved it to the Qingyang Palace "to make up for the relics of Laozi." On the base is a poem inscribed by Xinyangzi:

> The bronze sheep was obtained in the capital.
> I moved to Chengdu and set it in the ancient Taoist site.
> If Yin Xi can recognize this sheep,
> He should be happy to meet Laozi in Huayang.

Once again, it echoes the *Shu Ben Ji*.

Good things come in pairs. In year 9 of the Daoguang Reign (1829 CE), Zhang Ke's family in Chengdu invited Yunnan craftsmen Chen Wenbing and Gu Tiren to cast a double-horned bronze sheep and offer it to the Qingyang Palace. Soon, these two sheep became a treasure of the temple.

During the Guangxu period, Yamakawa Hayamizu, a Japanese teacher at the Sichuan Higher Education Institute, went to the Qingyang Palace to look for the bronze sheep with the words "Canmeige Zhenwan." But "there are many halls in the palace, where is the bronze sheep hidden now, searched many times but not found."

Yamakawa Hayamizu published *Bashu*, which is his Sichuan travelogue. In the same year, the *General Overview of Chengdu* was published. In this book, some information about the Qingyang Palace is introduced.

"There are two bronze sheep in the hall, not Tang Dynasty artifacts. They should be the smokers at the big official's house in the Ming Dynasty."

"The bronze sheep in the main hall of Qingyang Palace, with holes in its head, was a smoker in the homes of ancient nobles. Because the age is too long, all kinds of lies circulated, surprisingly, the absurd statement that touching the sheep can cure diseases."

The smoker should refer to the single-horned bronze sheep, some say it is from Yan Shifan's family in the Ming Dynasty, and some say it is from Jia Sidao's family in the Southern Song Dynasty, which is inconclusive. The most interesting example of the opposite of touching a bronze sheep can cure illness is found in the book *Ji Wo Can Zui* by Wang Kun, a scholar in the twenty-first year of the Daoguang Reign (1841): "There are two stone lions in the second hall of the Chengdu government office, which are made simply and are about three feet high. If someone touches its head, that person will have a headache; if he touches its body, he will have body pain."

In the twelfth year of the Republic of China (1923), Liu Shiliang wrote a bamboo lyric:

> The copper sheep is unique.
> Touch it, and you will be cured.
> There is a new way to get a boy.
> Use your hot hands to touch the sheep's cold belly.

And note: "Qingyang Palace is famous for its bronze sheep, and women superstitiously touch the belly of the sheep to have a boy." In addition to getting rid of diseases, touching the copper sheep has the effect of seeking a son.

CHAPTER 23

The Chengdu Markets in Twelve Months

International Exhibition Capital

It has now been proposed to make Chengdu a "World City of Culture and Innovation," "World City of Tourism," "World City of Events," "International Capital of Gastronomy," "International Capital of Music," and "International Capital of Exhibition." In ordinary times, this is to learn from and connect with the developed and advanced world, while in calendar time, many are a revival movement of the Tang and Song dynasties. For example, in Chengdu during the Song Dynasty, "The country was peaceful for a long time, and Chengdu was as prosperous as the capital" (Zhou Mi, Song Dynasty, *The Miscellaneous Knowledge of the Kuixin*), and every month there were large fairs or "commodity fairs" with different themes. To some extent, Chengdu was already considered the capital of the exhibition.

The name "Chengdu Markets in Twelve Months" was recorded by Governor Zhao Bian in the *Records of Ancient and Modern Chengdu*: "Lantern Market in the first lunar calendar month, Flower Market in the second, Silkworm Market in the third, Brocade Market in the fourth, Fan Market in the fifth, Incense Market in the sixth, Seven Treasures Market in the seventh, Osmanthus Market in the eighth, Medicine Market in the ninth, Wine Market in the tenth, Plum Market in the eleventh, and Peach Symbol Market in the twelfth." We can only search and examine Song Dynasty lyrics, poems, and other texts to splice and recover as many details as possible.

The Streets of Chengdu in the Song Dynasty

In Chengdu during the Song Dynasty, one had to walk through the streets to get to the daily and festival markets by car or on foot. Sometimes, the markets were simply held on the streets. It is conceivable that the roads, with their muddy strips and potholes, would still be bustling with red men and green women rushing to the market, allowing the city to reach the same level of prosperity as the capital.

> It is challenging to travel all over the world.
> Flavors in other places are mixed with sorrow and joy.

On the way to Guangxi, Fan Chengda wrote in his diary: Jiangxi "The road on the rotten mud like oil … bearer walking in the mud, … small steps are very difficult, exhausted." Hunan "road conditions very poor … potholes and mud, although there are a few days of sunshine, the shoes on the feet are still not dry, small steps beware of falling, the staff under the groaning can be heard." These kinds of records are sad records. In the poem *Staying at Pingchi Village in the Evening*, he writes:

> The mud on the road dried up
> And the hooves feel relaxed.
> The road is flat now,
> Just suitable for speeding up the march.

The poet has a sense of joy.

On the contrary, the hooves are heavy and slow once the rain and mud are wet. It took as long as five months to enter Chengdu, and the difficulty of the road can be imagined.

Perhaps because of the suffering of the mud road, Fan Chengda, ruling Shu at the beginning, proceeded to repair the streets of Chengdu. Previously, Zhang Tao, son of Senior Academician Zhang Gen, served as the Governor of Shu and had paved a brick and stone road for Chengdu in the 13th year of the Shaoxing Reign (1143), but it was only more than 2,000 *zhang* (about 6 kilometers) long

and did not solve the problem at the root. So, on top of this, Fan Chengda "…
selected artisans, respectively assigned management personnel. The whole process
was supervised well, and the project was held as scheduled. The government
paid all the road construction costs, and not a single penny was charged to the
people. And every day, they are also responsible for the production of food, so the
artisans are desperately hard working long before the road construction project
is completed. The road was 3,360 *zhang* long, using over two million bricks and
costing over 20 million in strings of copper coins. At the beginning and end of
each street, two stones were set up to distinguish the width of the road. There
were 14 such streets. Then, on the side of each street, promenades like the ones
popular in Jiangsu and Zhejiang were arranged. You won't be drenched when it
rains, and there will be no mud on the road when you ride a horse on the street.
The road surface is very flat, whether you walk slowly or quickly. The people of
Chengdu are very impressed: 'The newly repaired big road is just like Zhou Road.
Finally, we can see it with our own eyes.'"

The Zhou Dynasty had built an extensive and flat road between the capital of
the country, Haojing, and the eastern capital, Luoyi, which was called the "Zhou
Road." The people of Chengdu borrowed the phrase Zhou Road from the *Book
of Poetry* to describe and praise the 14 new streets built by Fan Chengda, which
shows that the public sentiment was high, and the hearts of the people were in
favor of them.

For these new streets, Fan Chengda was also quite proud of himself. In his
poem *On the Horse at the North Gate on the Second Day of the Third Month*, he
wrote:

> The newly renovated streets look like they've been scrubbed,
>
> the constant flow of carriages and riders going out to the streets.
>
> All kinds of flowers and trees are bright and colorful.
>
> The noblemen put them on their heads.
>
> Ten miles of the lively lot.
>
> The noblemen on the carriages drew up the beaded curtains
>
> And to see the lively scene.
>
> The stores were open.
>
> Chengdu was as prosperous as Yangzhou.

Most of these 14 specific street names are no longer available; now only know that there is the famous Stalagmite Street. Fan's poem *Visiting the Pagoda of Anfu Temple on the First Day of Bingshen* has two sentences about Stalagmite Street:

> Stalagmite New Street is a good place to have fun.
> I am happy with my people in the market.

The term *fengchang* is still used in the Sichuan dialect today, which means to visit a market.

In 2007, a street block site from the Tang to Song dynasties was discovered on the north side of Jiangnanguan Street in Jinjiang District of Chengdu, with a brick-paved street that stretches for dozens of meters and is rare in the history of Chinese urban archaeology. The pavement was built vertically with special long and thin bricks, with two types of masonry: "herringbone" and "zigzag." The middle of the pavement is slightly higher than the sides, and the pavement has apparent traces of wheel crushing and repair after-use damage. This may not be the one laid out by Fan Chengda, but it should be similar.

The Market of Twelve Months

The streets were renovated, various fairs were held at the same time, and "Chengdu" became a high-frequency word in the cultural reports of the Song Dynasty.

Based on the Sui and Tang dynasties, the Song Dynasty saw a considerable leap in the development of the commodity economy, with bazaars formed in the capital and local prefectures for exchanging goods and even a certain kind of bazaar specializing in a specific type of commodity. They were held as scheduled, enriching the people's food baskets and the literati's corpus. In the Northern Song Dynasty, Dongjing had a bamboo market. In the Southern Song Dynasty, Lin'an had a medicine market, a rice market, a meat market, a vegetable market, a flower market, a bead market, and a fresh fish market. Shaoxing Prefecture had nine markets, including the plum market and the market in front of Longxing Temple, and similarly, some of the Chengdu bazaars were held in front of the temple.

In comparison, Chengdu's thematic bazaars are the most numerous and comprehensive.

1. The lantern market in the first month of the lunar calendar

During the first month of the lunar calendar in the Song Dynasty, Chengdu had a lantern market where you could buy and sell lanterns and watch the lanterns in the street. Whether you were rich or poor, you'd be able to feast your eyes on it.

"In the second year of the Kaibao Reign of the Song Dynasty, the court ordered to set up the lanterns on three nights of the next year's Shangyuan Festival. Since then, it has become an annual practice. Every year, on the fourteenth, fifteenth, and sixteenth day of the first month, a large breakfast will be set up in the Daci Temple on these three days, and a banquet will be set up in the evening at the Five Gate Tower. After dinner, the guests will watch the lanterns hanging on the lantern scaffold together. The time when the lanterns were switched on and off is carried out according to the governor's wishes. It was a bustling and colorful scene. And Zhaojue Temple is the most prosperous place on the streetlights."

From the 14th day of the first month of the third year of the Kaibao Reign in the Northern Song Dynasty (970), officials and celebrities in Chengdu would gather in the morning for breakfast at the Daci Temple and dinner at the Five Gate Tower, where the lanterns were released at the beginning of the night (i.e., equivalent to 19:00 to 21:00). When to open the banquet. When to close the lanterns was all up to the governor of Chengdu, who opened a little earlier and closed a little later if he was happy. Otherwise, he opened and closed a little earlier. At that time, the color and shape of the lanterns constantly changed on the colorful hillside, and the sea of people around Zhaojue Temple was particularly festive.

The poem "Shangyuan Lantern Eve" by Tian Kuang, the Governor of Chengdu, described the lantern market in the first month of the lunar calendar:

> I gazed in the four directions,
> all were happy to play.
> Only in the whole Shu area
> the people and products were more prosperous than in other places.
> The precious lanterns were burning on a spring night.
> And the fragrance of smoke floated in the Jinli.
> People from all over the city came to see the lanterns.
> The endless lights stretched for thousands of miles.
> Beautiful women meet to see the lights.

Fragrant carriages were everywhere.

The sound of people rolling like a thunderclap, far out.

The lights on the trees were as many as the stars in the sky.

The drums blew and shook the earth with a clamor.

The bright moonlight shone on the earth like water.

There were joyful people everywhere,

I sat on a tall building for a long time to view the scene.

The hearts of the people were grateful to the emperor for his kindness.

The monks in the temple sang to the Buddha.

Everyone joined together and shouted blessings to the northeast,

May the emperor live forever, like a high mountain.

You can naturally hear the chants when you watch the lanterns in Daci Temple and Zhaojue Temple. Lu You's poem *Dingyou Shangyuan* described the lanterns in the Five Gate Tower:

Noisy gongs and drums reverberate through the gates five,

Ten-thousand lights glow on the Lantern Mountain as day turns to night.

Beauty and moon combine in a breathtaking sight,

As the guest folds the plum, his soul takes flight.

Lantern mountain refers to the night viewing of the changing lights of the mountain hut, a colorful hut built to celebrate the festival and shaped like a mountain towering overhead.

2. The flower market in the second month of the lunar calendar

During the Song Dynasty, Chengdu's flowers were known far and wide, and the most abundant, best, and most famous flowers were begonias. Song Qi once praised: "The begonias of Shu are really the most beautiful in the world."

Fan Chengda even said, "For the begonias alone, one should also come to Western Shu." Lu You was even crazier about the begonias in Chengdu. He praised it in his poem *Chengdu Walk*:

There are 100,000 begonias in Chengdu.

Their prosperity and splendor unmatched in the world.

This is no exaggeration and is highly consistent with the official narrative, such as the *Universal Geography of the Taiping Era*, which states, "Chengdu begonia trees are especially colorful." Interestingly, the flower market in Chengdu has been a regular market for many years.

It is not surprising that the flower market in the second month of the lunar calendar was rarely mentioned in the literature of the Song Dynasty. Xue Tian, a financial scholar and Governor of Yizhou in the Northern Song Dynasty, covered this in his poem *A Hundred Rhymes on the Book of Chengdu*:

> The beaded curtain of the willow embankment
> rolls up in the night moon,
> The spring breeze of the flower market
> embroiders the curtain.

The term "night moon" reminds us of Xiao Gou, who went into exile with Emperor Xizong of the Tang Dynasty in Chengdu. And he said, "The flower market is closed at night." Like other fairs, the flower market does not end until dusk.

The opening time of the flower market may be during the "Flower Festival," which is the birthday of the hundred flowers on the 12th or 15th days of the second lunar month. Perhaps it is more likely that the flower market was also held on the 15th day in the Song Dynasty, as it is recorded in *General Overview of Chengdu* that the people of Chengdu went to the Qingyang Palace Flower Fair on the 15th day of the second lunar month in the Qing Dynasty.

3. The silkworm market in the third month of the lunar calendar

"Every spring in the third lunar month, Sichuan would hold a silkworm market; by then, all kinds of merchants gathered, store trading was active, and Sichuan people praised its prosperous scene." A Song Dynasty poem expresses that "the people gather in department stores. The most important thing is to be timely in trading. They are taking advantage of this before plowing mulberry to help fund farming performance. There are so many goods. All the trivialities are not left out." The date and location of the third month sericulture market vary; see Chapter One "Chengdu, the Ancient Kingdom of Cancong" for details.

Su Shi (also called Su Dongpo) and his brothers are in harmony with the silkworm market. Here is Su Zhe's poetry on the silkworm market:

Withered mulberry leaves, like parched parchment, come to life
As new silkworms bask in the radiance of a clear day's light.
Tools of yesteryear are lost to memory and time,
But winter's clothes await the blossoming of spring's chime.
Sell the remaining grain with careful calculation,
And purchase silkworm equipment with hopeful expectation.
For not only women's boxes, but men's hoes gleam in the sun,
And all thoughts of play are gone, as kin and friends are as one.
The market brims with wine and food, the air alive with song,
As drums and flutes blend in chaotic harmony, all night long.
These customs, held dear in Cancong's reign, have long since passed,
But tradition's unbroken chain ensures they forever last.
Though I see no ancient customs in other lands or seas,
I hear the rustle of the pith, borne on the wind's gentle breeze.

Su Shi wrote a poem to follow his brother:

Shu people often suffer hardship in food and clothing,
Shu people do not want to go home
when they go out to play.
Thousands of people farm for the food
of tens of thousands of people,
After a year of hard work,
they can only rest in the spring.
During the farming season, silkworms are brought out
and traded at the market,
Everyone forgot about the hard work
and had a great time at the silkworm market.
Last year's frost affected the fall harvest.
This year, the equipment for raising silkworms is piling up.
The reeling tools are all laid out.
Everyone scrambles to buy the best silkworm seeds.

I remember when I was a child with my brother,
We dropped off our books yearly
and went to the markets and temples.
People in the market boast of their goods
and engage in fierce business competition.
The rural people are mute and
are cheated by treacherous merchants.
Your poem reminds me of the past.
I don't grieve leaving the capital,
but I suffer over the years we lost.

Su Shi's close friend monk Zhongshu also wrote "Silkworm Market," which follows the tune of *Memories of Jiangnan*.

Delighting in a visit to Chengdu,
Joyful in the silk world,
Hear the songs echo in the night.
Shining lights on the red tower
Have been invited by Spring.
Carriages and horses clog the streets in Yingzhou,
As the crowd moves away,
Silk merchants, blissful in the ring,
As slender willows sway with mulberry leaves.
My horse, without moving,
Watches the bustling scene …

4. The brocade market in the fourth month of the lunar calendar

As the Tang Dynasty poet Wei Zhuang wrote, "Jinli, silkworm market, full of pearls, millions of red makeups. Jade cicadas and golden sparrows, treasure bun flower clusters and pendant, embroidered clothes long." First, there are silkworms; then there is brocade. The silkworm market thrives on driving the development of brocade. Women bought silkworm ware in the silkworm market, weaved brocade, rinsed brocade, and went to the brocade market for trading. They were busy but did not wear a foot-and-a-half brocade. As the Southern Song Dynasty lyricist Wang Yuanliang's wrote in his poem *Silkworm Market*:

Chengdu's beauty is as white as frost.

They went to pick mulberry with their baskets.

After a year of raising silkworm seedlings,

they could only produce a little silk.

How can they make clothes for themselves

with this bit of silk?

Although in the Song Dynasty, "Sichuan was rich, and the silk and brocade were the first in the country" and "there were too many brocade machines and jade workers," (*The Biography of the Song Dynasty*, Volume 35) the fate of brocade weavers was still sad.

Song Dynasty lyrics and poems have a lot to say about the "silkworm market" but not a word about the "brocade market." There are no other records of the "brocade market" in Song Dynasty literature, except in the *Records of Ancient and Modern Chengdu*.

5. The fan market in the fifth month of the lunar calendar

"Every year on the fifth month of the lunar calendar, the people of Chengdu go to the street in front of Daci Temple to buy fans, and this street is called the fan market." Although this is the record of the *Chronicles of Huayang County* in the Jiaqing Reign of the Qing Dynasty, I think the Song Dynasty was almost the same. The fifth month of the lunar calendar has entered the mid-summer, the fan has become an excellent necessity, so the fan market in response to the time and rise. Fan market, "Shu fan" or "Sichuan fan" should be the main commodity.

"Poly bone fan, besides Jiangsu's production, is the best fan in Sichuan. The delicate fan is suitable for the scholar, gorgeous fan is suitable for beautiful women."

6. The incense market in the sixth month of the lunar calendar

In June, Chengdu has an incense market. It is the merchant trading incense place. There were many temples and palaces in Chengdu during the Song Dynasty, and the amount of incense was huge, so with the centralized supply of the incense market, more was needed.

7. The seven-treasures market in the seventh month of the lunar calendar

Seven treasures refer to department stores. The *Exhausting Overview of All Parts of the Empire* records: "In the fifth month, selling incense and herbs in Guanjie is a medicine market. The market of seven treasures is where all kinds of utensils are sold." If this record is correct, then the seven-treasures market should be at Guanjie in Chengdu in the fifth month every year.

In the Ming Dynasty, there was another saying: "In winter, in front of the Daci Temple, various utensils are sold in the seven-treasures market." I wonder if this was the case in the Song Dynasty.

8. The osmanthus market in the eighth month of the lunar calendar

Seasonal rotation, once in the eighth month, Chengdu City will have the fragrance of osmanthus, and osmanthus is a widely used held osmanthus market. It is logical.

The laurel trees in Xindu are particularly abundant, "Every autumn, when the osmanthus blossoms, it can produce more than a few hundred quintals. Businessmen in the tea and candy industry from various towns come here to buy." However, this is the situation in the Qing Dynasty. Still, I am afraid that the Song Dynasty in Chengdu's osmanthus market is also for the similar need to purchase many osmanthuses and the rise.

9. The medicine market in the ninth month of the lunar calendar

Among the twelve markets, the medicine market in Chengdu during the Song Dynasty was the most famous. Just as the *History of the Song Dynasty · The Chronicles of Geography* records, "The people of Chengdu worked so hard that not an inch of land was barren, and there were three to four large harvests each year. The proceeds were mostly used for trips and purchases, and the number of people going out for fun was particularly high, and fairs such as medicine markets were very well developed. Such behavior was engaged in for months at a time."

Yang Yi (974–1020 CE) records in his *Yang Wengong Tanyuan*: "Yizhou has a medicine market. It is held every year on the seventh day of the seventh month of the lunar calendar, with guests from all directions. The medicine market has a large variety of drugs, and the amount is huge. The trade takes three days to end.

Those in need go to the market to buy medicines.

During the Chunhua period, Cui Mai, an adviser official, was appointed as the transfer agent of the Gorge Road. Cui Mai was weak, and he had a pillow made of cypress. He ordered to spend 10,000 coins to buy hundreds of medicines in the medicine market. For each medicine, he took a small amount and put it inside the pillow for the various points of the head so that the smell of the medicine would thoroughly incense itself. After lying this way for several months, his skin ulcerated extensively, eyebrows and beard had fallen off, and Cui Mai was so angry that he threw himself into the river. Some say it is the drug fumigated between the hair and bone joints, resulting in skin disease."

More than a hundred medicinal products are all over the market, so the Chengdu medicine market has quite a complete range of drugs. Song Qi was visiting the medicine market and saw "Peonies and rhubarb piled up like mountains and their fragrance overflowed the market." Zhang Shinan was playing in the medicine market, and even saw the "rhinoceros" from the Li, Ya, Xihe, and Dangchang people, and other minorities. In addition, there was a proprietary Chinese medicine called "detoxification pills." The price is 1,000 copper coins per pill. Cai Tao recorded the unique sales of this medicine in *Tiewei Shan Cong Tan*: "In the past in Chengdu, a bazaar was held every year at the Duanwu and Chongyang festivals at the Daci Temple, gathering many merchants with goods. Various goods were sold in the bazaar, also known as the medicine market. So, someone shouted "medicine for sale" between the windows. The buyer knew what it meant and hurriedly threw in a thousand coins, so he got a pill from the window called "deciphering pills"; just one pill could save a life." It seems that in the fifth month, not only the fan market but there is also the medicine market.

Song Qi's poem, *The Medicine Market on the Ninth*, clearly explains the medicine market and Chengdu's climate:

> Chrysanthemum Day, a festival grand,
> Inviting all to roam free across the land.
> The medicine market teems with a bustling throng,
> Scented herbs on display, their magic strong.
> In baskets, remedies aplenty, cures for pain,
> Comforting the sick and easing their woe and strain.
> This time of year, when prices are within reach,
> The need to buy and sell meets mutual speech.

Cao Zhi, always wary of the false and the fake,
While Han Kang sold at stable prices, no need to take.
In the southwest, plagues are common, with each passing year,
Amid humid spring and summer, good medicine brings cheer.
A thousand coins of heavy weight, fitting tribute to pay,
To the sellers who provide hope, to light up a new day.
For officials and common folk, health is a shared need,
Medicine the magic cure that allows us to lead.
My heart is moved, to reflect and to sigh,
In the power of medicine, to heal and to defy.

Lu You thought in his *Notes of Lao Xue'an*: "The largest medicine market in Chengdu is held on the ninth day of the ninth month at the Yuju Shrine. The *Yang Wen Gong Tan Yuan* says it is the seventh day of the seventh month, which is wrong." The *Yang Wen Gong Tan Yuan* records that the bazaar will be held for three days. Zhuang Chuo (c. 1079–?) has different states in his *Jilei Bian*: "When the medicine market was held on the ninth day of the ninth month, people set up stores from outside the Qiao Gate to the Yuju Shrine and the five gates to sell all kinds of medicinal materials. There were piles of rhinoceros horns, musk, and other goods, and military officials such as the governor and the superintendent came to see them. They also set up a large wine dzong under the five gates, which could hold dozens of bushels, and prepared all kinds of wine cups, so that all famous Taoists could drink freely. Such a medicine market was to be held for five days." This is how Jing Tang's lyric *Flowers in the Rain · Chrysanthemum* was written:

In front of the Yuju Shrine and by the Tonghu Pavilion,
the medicine market of Chengdu is competing.
The purple cornelian decorates the seats,
and the yellow chrysanthemum floats the goblets.
The lanes and alleys are linked and bridled.
The people on the stairs were playing music.
Looking up to the sky, it is a year of good scenery
and a good day on the ninth.
I pity myself as a traveler and look at the guests,
Is the reason for lingering here because of greed?

Who would have thought that my heart has come to the North Palace
and that my delight, too, is in the East?
I am sorry for the farewell.
I have yet to rush to the prow.
We drank with beauty and had fun.
Next year's conference will be held in another place,
just like today, but we will miss each other because of it.

In the ninth year of the Qiandao Reign (1173 CE), when Lu You first came to Chengdu from Nanzheng, he wrote the lyrics of *Han Gong Chun*:

Hunting and practicing martial arts of the treacherous ancient bases
and on the vast flat rivers.
Carry a bow and arrow, arm waving eagle, hand-tied to the tiger.
Until the twilight, the sound of reed, only to return from the hunt,
the camp tent on the green felt had long been full of thick snowflakes.
After drinking wine, and waving a pen, that dragon-flying cursive,
ink dripping, fell on the paper.
People may be wrong to praise me,
it is a poetic feeling, but it also has a general strategy of the super talent.
Why did I leave the Nanzheng front to come south to Chengdu?
Was it to visit the medicine market at the Chongyang Festival
and see the lantern mountain at the Lantern Festival?
Whenever the flowers bloom and thousands of people play,
I wear a hat diagonally, carrying a whip, and let the horse roam.
Whenever I listened to the songs and dances,
I would think of my past military life and feel many emotions,
unconsciously spilling tears in front of the wine bottle.
Please always remember,
kill the enemy to serve the country,
to build an incredible feat to be a marquis is to struggle,
I do not believe that this is all arranged by god.

In Lu You's mind, the Chongyang Medicine Market, like the Lantern Hill on New Year's Eve, was a momentary event in Chengdu and the most personalized business card event in the city.

A poem written by Su Shi in the autumn of the ninth year of the Xining Reign (1076 CE) to celebrate the victory, *He Man Zi · A Lyric from Mizhou to Feng Dang Shi, the Governor of Yizhou*, mentions that the governor of Chengdu would also visit the medicine market in private and in civilian clothes, in addition to participating in the Wanhua River tour.

At that time, Feng Danshi, the governor of Chengdu, put down the rebellion of the minority in Maozhou, and Su Shi wrote this piece as a gift after hearing the news. Among Dongpo's 300-odd lyrics, this is the only one about current and important events. It is also scarce among traditional euphemisms.

I heard people say that the Min and E mountains
before the pacification of the chaos.
The hills and the landscape are bleak.
But now, rumors of the pacification of the Yangtze River,
Everything is clear.
I feel that the autumn sends a refreshing breeze,
just in time for a dream to return home.
Fortunately, you are in the southwest fortification,
Building the Great Wall is as strong as the iron bronze wall.
Although in the political affairs hall,
you are the youngest of the three councillors,
and now,
the southwest barbaric areas have been peaceful
after the pacification of the rebellion.
Don't let down the excellent scenery of the flower stream;
you can enjoy it as much as you like.
The medicine market in Chengdu is booming,
so why not visit the market and travel lightly?
Ask Zhuo Wenjun, who used to be a shopkeeper,
if she is still there today.
With your appreciation of the tour,
the famous places there will be worthwhile.
I think you should have some joy and pride in your heart
when you sing the new song of praise by Wang Bao.

This poem refers to the Chongyang Medicine Market as one of the liveliest festivals in Chengdu, the Flower Stream, which is the same as Xue Tian's poem:

> The scenery of the medicine market
> is beyond the insect sting,
> the flower pools are roaming,
> and the joy is before the sound of birdsong.

And it is like Lu You's poem on the medicine market and New Year's Eve. In Chengdu in the Song Dynasty, the medicine market was not only a big market but also a big gathering for all people to enjoy: "At dawn, all the herbs and exotics produced in Sichuan were gathered with the Taoists, and the governor set up a banquet in the medicine market to have fun with the people. He gave special wine to the Taoists to reward them. Early that morning, all the local people of Chengdu came to the market, and it was said that the medicinal qi inhaled in the market could cure diseases and bring health to people." The governor set up wine in the market for fun, not a covert action, but a public event.

If the weather conditions are not good, the people in the market will not be unhappy because they believe that if it rains on this day, the immortals are in it. Therefore, Zhongshu wrote a lyric:

> Chengdu is good, the medicine market is leisurely.
> Step out of the five gates to sound the sword pendant
> and not climb three islands to see the gods.
> The misty knotted spirit smoke.
> In the shadow of the clouds, songs blow through the warm frosty sky.
> Why use chrysanthemum flowers to float jade wine,
> I would like to ask the vermilion grass into a golden elixir.
> One capsule will fix a long life.

10. *The wine market in the tenth month of the lunar calendar*

Chengdu has been producing wine since ancient times, with many brands and large quantities, so it is common to have a particular wine market. Lu You wrote a poem, *Writing Poetry While Drunk Upstairs*:

The natural man should not waste his life,

I was going to destroy the bandits to recover the country.

I never thought my life would be so wasted.

My youth withered for eight years in Yizhou.

In the middle of the night,

I touched my pillow and suddenly screamed.

In the dream, I recovered Songting Pass.

It is lamentable that the opportunity

to recover the Central Plains has been lost repeatedly.

I will shed tears again when I drink tomorrow.

The wine in the official building of Yizhou is like the sea.

I came to the wine flag every day to buy wine.

I drank too much and started gambling, just for fun.

I casually rolled the dice and won,

and there was applause all around.

My gaze was sharp and murderous.

After a gambling spree, I felt that I was not a maniac.

How dare I forget our ancient capital

with the ancestral temple of the emperor.

The deity of the ancestors is at the side of the emperor.

It is not a bragging point that the wine in the office building of Yizhou was like a sea. According to statistics, at the end of Song Gaozong's reign, the annual tax revenue of the national wine was 14 million copper coins, and the Sichuan wine tax was 4.1–6.9 million, accounting for 29% to 49% of the revenue of the national wine tax.

11. The plum market in the eleventh month of the lunar calendar

There is now a month-long "Plum Blossom Cultural Festival" in Chengdu, and people sell wax plums with branches on the street. Chengdu people have loved plums since ancient times, so a plum market came into being. If you stay in Chengdu for a long time, you will also develop a plum fetish, such as Lu You, who had an eight-year career in Yizhou.

When I was walking in the west of Chengdu,
I was once drunk with plum blossoms.
The fragrance of the plum blossoms was constant.
From the Qingyang Palace to Wanhua Stream.

12. The peach symbol market in the twelfth month of the lunar calendar

The Complete Tang Poems has one poem titled the *Peach Symbol of Meng Shu Era*. It has two lines:

The New Year is celebrated warmly.
The festival is called Long Spring.

An exhibit at the Chengdu Museum says, "This couplet is the first Chinese New Year couplet in history and is said to have been written by the Later Shu Emperor Meng Chang on New Year's Eve in 964 CE." This saying is not accurate enough. According to Ruan Yue's *Zengxiu Shihua Zonggui*, Volume 31, which quoted *Tan Yuan*, Xing Yinxun was a native of Chengdu. He served as a Grand Consular in the Later Shu regime. Before the imperial army was about to crush Later Shu, just in time for New Year's Eve, the Emperor of Later Shu, Meng Chang, ordered him to write two lines of poetry on a peach charm. He wrote the above two verses. In the following year, in 965 CE, the Later Shu fell. He surrendered to the Song Dynasty and was appreciated by Song Taizu. As Yang Yi (974–1020 CE), the author of the *Tan Yuan*, lived near to the time of Later Shu, his account should be credible, and Xing Yinxun was the original author of this spring couplet.

It is not surprising that Chengdu has a peach charm market. At the end of the year, everyone went to the market to buy spring couplets and stick them at home so that they could prepare for the Spring Festival and New Year's Eve. In *General Overview of Chengdu* is recorded that the custom of "sticking spring couplets" was observed in Chengdu on the 30th day of the twelfth month during the Qing Dynasty, which should have been long ago.

Postscript

———— ◦◆◦ ————

There are too many exaggerated stories and speculations about Chengdu's history and culture circulating in the public and online spheres. Most reports are not written based on the original documents, or not checked, or checked without textual research, and the result is wrong, even sometimes the way the check needs to be corrected. For example, the Japanese scholar Yamakawa Hayasui wrote in his book *Bashu* that "*Han Zhi* recorded, 'After the Qin State unified the country, the Jiangshui Shrine was built in Shu.' Since then, the Jiangdu Temple was founded in Sichuan." *Han Zhi* is the *Book of Han · Treatise on Sacrifices*. A similar sentence is quoted in the *Universal Geography of the Taiping Era, Exhausting Overview of All Parts of the Empire, Broad Records of Shu, Chronicles of Unification of the Qing Dynasty*, and *A Study of the Monuments of Chengdu City and Lanes*. But this is not true of the original text of "Treatise on Sacrifices." In Tang Dynasty, "Treatise Extended to All Regions" recorded "Jiangdu Shrine was in the south of eight *li* of Chengdu County, Yizhou. Qin merged into the country and set up the Jiangshui Shrine in Shu." Perhaps this is the earliest etymology. The recent writings often follow *A Study of the Monuments of Chengdu City and Lane*, describing that "Qin merged the country and set up Jiangdu Temple in Shu." And believe it is the original text of the *Book of Han*. This is ridiculous and pathetic.

The poet Du Jun commented on my book *Chengdu in the Ancient Books*, saying, "The ancient books are the sources, origins, and topics of the conversation. It shows what the author says has its source." There is a layer of emotion in this book's title. Most of the famous places and monuments in Chengdu have been left with a false name, and their true faces are only partially preserved within the ancient books, especially those relics that could have been preserved but were eventually destroyed by man, which is most saddening. This book is still the same. 99% of the references are original documents; some are even the first references in the respective fields.

However, sometimes I will use the citation occasionally for convenience. For example, the chapter "Chengdu, the Ancient Kingdom of Cancong" and the *Chronicles of Huayang* cite one sentence from the *Chronicles of Qionglai County*; the edition I reviewed was printed in the eleventh year of the Republic of China. And there are no sayings like "The idol should follow the appearance of Cancong." Shénxiàng 神象 should be shénxiàng 神像, the image of god. I knew there was a mistake, but I quoted it as usual and didn't bother to change it. See the article "Sanxingdui and the 'Forever God' of the Shu People," which mentioned the original text of the *Chronicle of Qionglai County* for comparison. Besides doubt, it was also done deliberately to take care of the sense of speech and to save expression. Of course, more of the quotations stand up to verification.

Compared with *Chengdu in the Ancient Books*, this book has more academic chapters. For example, the article *Dujiangyan before 'Dujiangyan'* unpacks the primary literature on Li Bing and Dujiangyan and puts forward several original ideas. It was initially published in the twelfth series in the *Journal of Local Culture Studies* (Sichuan University Press, 2017). Now it has been substantially revised to include in this book. The reader who wants to cite it, please refer to this version.

Another example is the article *Interpretation of the Shooting and Harvest Portrait Brick*, which reviews the gains and losses of previous scholars and provides a new logical and self-consistent interpretation. This article was originally published in the *Chengdu Evening News* on October 22, 2018, entitled "A New Detailed Interpretation of the Shooting and Harvest Portrait Brick in East Han Dynasty." This time, the original title is restored, and several articles are added, an academic practice of "additional evidence of famous objects" advocated by famed author Shen Congwen.

However, most of the articles in this book are still mainly for popularizing the ancient history of Chengdu. In this way, it can be regarded as a sister to *Chengdu in the Ancient Books*, but with a narrower period: it is roughly divided into two parts, with Li Bing governing Shu as the boundary (because of his governance of Shu and water, Yizhou became the capital of heaven); the period discussed is dominated by the ancient Shu and the two Han dynasties. Meanwhile, the "Past

Life of Qingyang Palace" and the "Chengdu Markets in Twelve Months" are used as backdrops. This book will help readers glimpse Chengdu in the Tang and Song dynasties and its origin.

The history of Chengdu is like Mount Min, which has been unbroken for a thousand years, and the relevant literature is like the Wen River, which is inexhaustible, so such a complex and valuable popularization work needs more people to take part and continue. I hope this small book is a new beginning. As one poem says:

> Reluctantly cast for tiles and bricks,
> Eventually, a reward of golden pearls.

Index

---◆◆---

Zhang Yi, 27, 29, 47, 50, 51, 57, 73, 74
Zhao Bian, 98, 158
Zhao, State of, 42, 134, 142
Zhao Xu, 98
Zheng Guo, 44, 55, 83
Zheng Guo's Canal, 44
Zhongshu, 7, 166, 173
Zhou Dynasty, 4, 15, 16, 56, 59, 154, 155, 160

Eastern Zhou, 4, 5, 15
Western Zhou, 16, 31
Zhuangzi, xii, 113
Zhuge Liang, 9, 43, 62, 113, 114
Zhu Mu, 6, 71, 72
Zhuo family, 42, 142
Zhu Xi, 91, 92, 93, 100
Zuo Si, xii, xiii, 19, 21, 59, 142, 144

ABOUT THE AUTHOR

Mr. Lin Ganqiu, the pen name of Zhu Jianbo, is a writer contracted by the Chengdu Literature Institute and a member of the Sichuan Writers Association. He has published monographs such as *Animals in the Book of Poetry*, *Seven Days of National Studies*, *An Appreciation of Women's Fiction*, *Chengdu in Ancient Books*, *The Lonely Journey to the End of the World: Selected Writings of Lin Ganqiu*, and others.